The Ancient Science of
GEOMANCY

Living in harmony with the earth

NIGEL PENNICK

with 128 illustrations

CRCS PUBLICATIONS
Post Office Box 1460
Sebastopol, California 95472

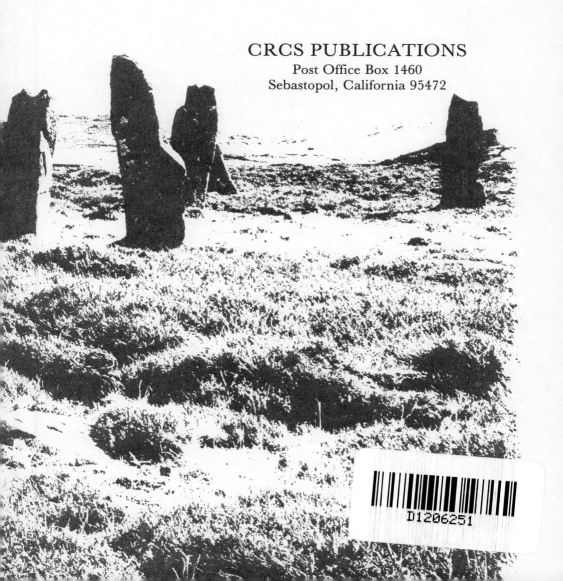

To Ann

Title-page:
Callanish, Isle of Lewis, a
megalithic observatory of
exceptional precision.

Library of Congress Cataloging-in-Publication Data

Pennick, Nigel.
    The ancient science of geomancy.

    Bibliography: p.
    Includes index.
    1. Geomancy. I. Title.
BF1773.P45 1987   133.3'33   87-7046
ISBN 0-916360-38-5

Published in Great Britain by Thames and Hudson Ltd.

INTERNATIONAL STANDARD BOOK NUMBER: 0-916360-38-5

Published in the United States by CRCS Publications

Distributed in the United States & Canada by
CRCS Publications

Contents

AUTHOR'S NOTE
In writing this book, I have attempted to deal with a subject which in modern jargon would be called 'interdisciplinary'. Themes and concepts from architecture, geometry, geography, cosmology, art, archaeology, metrology, numerology, astronomy, astrology, surveying, religion and mythology, all complex subjects in their own right, can be seen to have a common root in certain ancient practices which related them to a special place, time, cosmic position and purpose.

Evidence from a great number of sources indicates that there is certainly something linking all these enigmatic facts and universal practices, an age-old and venerable science which may be called geomancy. This system of belief and activity, although obliterated in the West, still survives in some other places, and can give us insight into such disparate and puzzling phenomena as the siting of churches, the alignments of sacred buildings, mystical geometry, earth effigies, holy wells, early city planning, and the omphalos.

I have tried to demonstrate the interconnection between these and other products of the sacred history of mankind, drawing on the researches of many who have dedicated their lives to the discovery of the key to the ancient, largely lost art of geomancy.

Nigel Pennick

Introduction

In modern times, people have lost their intimate connection with the earth. Most would tend to dismiss as needlessly esoteric the concept of harmony with the natural environment, and such a concept is indeed at variance with the philosophy of domination over the natural world inherent in modern technical civilization.

However, the practice of geomancy, which may roughly be defined as the science of putting human habitats and activities into harmony with the visible and invisible world around us, was at one time universal, and vestiges of it remain in the landscape, architecture, ritual and folklore of almost all countries in the world. This remarkable series of correspondences between different cultures has been held to be evidence for a former world civilization, perhaps that of the legendary Atlantis. But the fact that certain patterns and themes which are found in geomancy, for example the unicursal labyrinth, occur also in dreams and visions, suggests that they represent parts of the subconscious mind of mankind rather than a directly transmitted tradition. These archetypal patterns, integrated with the observed phenomena of earth and heavens, have produced the worldwide concurrence of outward form and inner purpose found in geomancy. Hence the seeking of cosmic power points on the surface of the earth, special places where the mind can expand into new levels of consciousness, places where visions, transcendental states of prophecy may be experienced.

Although geomancy and its effects have been largely destroyed in the West, enough remains to have enabled researchers past and present to reconstruct survivals elsewhere, to gain an insight into the ethos behind the practice.

To our ancestors, the properties of the earth were understood – and used. That the land is an awesome living complex to be tampered with at our peril is something which modern ecologists have brought back into our consciousness, and we can only hope that the message will be understood before we have reached the point of no return. Our forbears, directly dependent upon the earth and its forces, revered stream and fountain, rock and grove, not as gods in themselves, as later theists imagine, but as inherent sources of the spirits of the earth such as the Yarthlings and Hyter Sprites still talked of in East Anglian folklore.

The mysteries of geomancy were intimately linked with the soil by which one is nourished and to which one returns at death. It was directly concerned with the propagation of fertility, the cycles of the seasons, the calendar, the sources of water, and the positioning of fields. Many aspects of geomancy may now superficially appear to be little more than practical measures taken to ensure the most favourable water supply or the best aspect of the sun, but to regard the subject as an early form of town planning or farm management is to miss the point, by viewing it through the eyes of the modern technological world.

In geomancy, the world was conceived as a continuum in which all acts, natural and supernatural, conscious and unconscious, were linked in a subtle manner, one with the next. In this world view, the incorrect performance of an act, such as misorientating a building, was not merely doomed to fail in achieving its desired objective, but would also bring unforeseen and uncontrollable consequences. Conversely, if the correct manner was applied at the right place and time, the procedures would reflect not only what had gone before, but also what was about to happen. This philosophy underlies the Tarot, the I Ching, the Malagasy Sikidy, and numerous other forms of divination involving the creation of patterns to foretell the future. The beans, stones, yarrow stalks or cards assume patterns according to the influences pertaining in the universe at that moment, and consequently were

Chinese geomancy (Feng-Shui) is illustrated in the 'dragon veins' of a landscape by Huang Kung-wang, Yüan dynasty (1269–1354).

believed to be a significant reflection on the states then extant. In the same way, the positioning of houses or temples had to be done so as to reflect the state of the universe at the time they were founded, to be in harmony with the cosmic order, and not to disrupt the finely tuned balance.

The geomancy of a building, if constructed according to the correct principles, could be read by an initiate and may still be apparent to a modern researcher. Its orientation can be measured against sunrise alignments or magnetic variation (see p. 109), which may be used to date it fairly exactly. Its purpose and symbolic function can be determined by its geometry and metrology, and its relationship with other sacred structures can be worked out using modern mapping techniques.

So-called primitive societies still live as far as possible in a world patterned on the above lines, and, even in England today the earth spirit, *genius loci* or Yarthling is placated by a traditional offering in the ceremonies of laying foundation stones and topping-out. In the former, coins are often deposited beneath the stone, a custom which may find a parallel in the Brazilian practice of paying a voodoo witch doctor to sacrifice chickens at such a ceremony. The underlying beliefs, whether consciously practised or dismissed as mere tradition, are to do with the maintenance of the universe's harmony, and the keeping of cosmic order.

The intrinsic geometry underlying all material things is the basis for geomantic architecture, which is

Sunrise at Stonehenge. At Midsummer the rising sun can be seen from the centre of the circle over the pointed Heelstone.

required to harmonize with its purpose and position on the surface of the planet. Between geomantically determined sites, the alignments rediscovered by researchers like Black, Bennett, Watkins and Heinsch appear to have been known under different names to different cultures: the spirit paths or *lung-mei* of Chinese geomancy (Feng-Shui); the fairy roads of Ireland; the Royal Roads of England, etc. This geometry has been a subject of meditation for initiates of many religions; it underlies the sacred art of every great faith; it can be detected in molecular structures, in the scales on microscopic algae and protozoa, in the formation of stars, in the patterns on the surface of boiling liquids, and in the crystalline forms of minerals and ice. It is, in short, the universal means by which the intrinsic oneness of the universe may be comprehended.

The evidence of symbolism shows us that a sympathetic system once operated on many levels, from the local wise man or woman channelling away the harmful influences from a malevolently charged stone, to the priest-king performing his offices at the central national shrine, a multi-level hierarchy of cross-reinforcing rituals intended to sustain the cosmic order. This hierarchical structure was based on the concept of macrocosm and microcosm, the lesser reflecting in its constitution the greater.

Natural geomancy

One generation passeth away, and another generation
cometh:
but the earth abideth for ever.

Ecclesiastes, I, 4

It has frequently been observed that in many species of
animal a remarkable rapport exists between the
individual creature and its surroundings. This rapport
appears strange to modern people because they are now
far removed from the natural world. To us, the ability
of a pigeon to 'home' from hundreds of miles away, or
of a salmon to return to its birthplace from halfway
round the world in order to breed, is an extraordinary
and inexplicable phenomenon. But in nature such feats
are commonplace. Wild creatures inherently possess
these faculties, which science chooses to file away under

*Annual migrations of animal
herds in harmony with the seasons
show their integration with the
natural condition of the world.*

the heading 'instinct'. To the swallow, returning to the previous year's nesting site after a 15,000-mile round trip presents no problem – it just does it. The pigeon, the salmon, the swallow and every other wild creature, all are integrated with the environment. All acts are natural, and in accord with the animal's position in the biosphere. Only mankind is different – now.

Like the animal kingdom, early man was integrated with the environment, occupying his niche in a completely natural and unconscious manner. His life was controlled by the passage of the seasons, his nomadic wanderings on the face of the globe directed by necessity. The faculty now known as intuition was his guiding principle. It led him to find water, nourishment and shelter. It enabled him to sense the presence of danger and to avoid it. His symbiotic relationship with the 'ecosystem' was not yet broken. Possessing intelligence, he recognized his dependence upon Mother Earth, who had brought him into being and sustained him. She was the universal deity. Each part of her was therefore sacred, suffused with her spirit and manifest in differing forms according to the place. The various powers present in rocks, hills, trees, springs and rivers were operative and available at the appropriate times.

To such people, any alteration of the earth was unthinkable sacrilege. The early nomads left the land as they found it, spontaneously receiving whatever was given. Like some modern dowsers, ancient peoples were able directly to experience the energies in the earth, and attributed them to the activity of the earth spirit. The places where they occurred became sites of special reverence, later to be incorporated as the active sites in sacred buildings. But in the earliest times their numinous quality was directly perceived without need for images or ritual, which are the products of settled, organized religion. A natural reverence, alien to the modern spirit, guarded and nurtured these sites where anyone could experience his or her own direct magical relationship with the essential nature of the earth.

In later times, this pristine state of direct experience was to be seen in terms of a former Golden Age. In this primeval period, man the nomadic hunter-gatherer developed the first skills which started him on the path to civilization. The discovery of fire and the use of tools automatically altered his place in the natural order. He was now able to modify what nature provided and, to an ever-increasing extent, his own immediate environment.

Even more revolutionary was the domestication of animals, which at a stroke removed man's dependence on hunting, since a regular supply of food was thereby ensured. The prime objective now became the need to find suitable grazing land for the livestock. Of necessity, the ancient herdsman was still nomadic, moving from place to place with the cycles of the seasons. Regular patterns, marked out by the animals, and still integrated with the earth's energies, visited the special places which, it was believed, determined the fertility of the land and herds.

The old integration was now in decline. Man by his own ingenuity had removed himself from the position of a passive element in the ecosystem. He was transformed into its master, in conflict with the natural order. The original nomadic life had left little mark on the body of Mother Earth. It was only with the beginnings of settled life that any permanent impressions began to be made on the landscape. While some settlement had already taken place with lakeside or seaside fishing communities, its main impetus was the discovery, or invention, of agriculture.

Like the change from hunter to herdsman, the transition from nomad to settler was a radical alteration in life style, and with the change came a profound alteration in psychological outlook. Settled life necessitated the enclosure of space, a stopping of the free flow of the spirit of the earth, and the enclosed space required protection against intrusion. Instead of the whole word as his terrain, man's dominion was now confined to a small and precisely defined locality.

Nomadic tribes to this day follow certain cyclic routes in accordance with the seasons. Camps are made on traditional sites, and fairs and festivals occur at fixed places and times.

Settlement involved an irreversible disruption of the natural order, which would have been seen as potentially hazardous unless the earth were appeased. Clearing the forest and enclosing open land were seen as serious affronts to Mother Earth, while ploughing, digging boundary ditches, and even taking water from springs, would have been thought to affect the earth forces. To counter these offences against the natural state of the earth, appeasement was necessary, and sacrifice was made to ward off any possible ill effects of the project in hand. As the special places formerly visited by the nomads were no longer accessible to a settled population, the special places within the locality were elevated in importance. Their energies were no longer attributed to the activities of a worldwide spirit, but to individual spirits believed to inhabit the sites much as hermit crabs inhabit seashells. The sites themselves became the sacred areas of the settlement – local shrines which were resorted to at special times of the year when they were active.

Of particular importance to a farming community was an unfailing supply of water. Once discovered, such a supply had to be jealously guarded against pollution, drought or denial of access. It was thought that the appropriation of the waters of a spring involved the need to placate its spirit lest the privilege should be withdrawn.

Worship and sacrifice were therefore performed at springs, and later, by association, at man-made wells. In some places these rites grew in complexity, and in later times the sites became important shrines of the religions which arose.

The belief in sacrifice has been worldwide. The foundations of buildings, which were considered to profane the natural state of the world by artificially enclosing space, were always made secure by the offering of a blood sacrifice. If the natural wanderings of the earth's spirit were to be curtailed without ill effect, then a life had to be offered in exchange. This encroachment of the spirit's freedom was the first step on the road to urbanization – the remoulding of the earth in man's image.

During the long period when humanity's life style was solely agricultural, a set of practices and rituals grew up – now known under the name of nature religion. Medieval churchmen saw this set of beliefs as witchcraft, and attempted to stamp it out. Nineteenth-century theists saw nature religion as primitive spiritism. Modern times view it as superstition – which it is, in the true meaning of the word: something which 'stands over' from a previous era.

Nature religion involves rituals and techniques at certain classes of natural sites, all of which have special properties, whether therapeutic, oracular or fertility-inducing. All these classes of site have been appropriated by the essentially urban, patriarchal religions which have followed.

The sites whose spirits were evoked in nature religion were those untouched by human activity: springs, trees, hills, unworked stones, rocks, caves and rivers; places where the spirit of Mother Earth was manifested. Honoured by continuous traditional use, these sites have remained sanctified up to the present day, though sometimes in unlikely guises.

Springs and wells

Springs, places where streams spontaneously bubble forth from the ground, the birthplaces of rivers, provide one of the fundamental necessities of life, so it was natural that a visible source of water should be held in special reverence by early peoples as a place where the earth had blessed her children with one of her life-giving properties. And underground springs, detectable by dowsing, exhibit strong energies which were attributed in earlier times to the activity of spirit.

Apart from their life-giving properties, springs and their artificial counterparts, wells, have been resorted to since ancient times for the promotion of fertility, the cure of illness, and the gift of prophecy. At certain times of year, so it was believed, the spirits of springs could be invoked to achieve the desired result: fertile families, healthy bodies, or knowledge of the future.

Nature religion has survived into modern times in the form of habit and superstition, despite repeated attempts to stamp it out. All over Europe there are wells which bear the names of Christian saints, but whose sanctity is rooted in the earlier religion of nature. As with nearly all other classes of sacred sites, the Christian Church drew wells and springs into its sphere of influence so that they would not remain centres of the old religion, but would help disseminate the new. The old uses continued, however, despite numerous edicts and prohibitions issued at irregular intervals by pious Christian leaders. St Eligius, bishop of Noyon, and Edgar, Egbert and Cnut, kings of England, all issued specific prohibitions against worship at wells. Despite these edicts the practices survived largely intact into an era when they were noted and recorded before

Source of the River Kennet, this seasonally flowing spring was very probably regarded by our earliest ancestors as the residence of spirit, later to be commemorated by the magnificent neolithic monuments of Avebury parish.

St Ceriol's well, Penmon Priory, Wales. Holy wells in Britain are almost invariably associated with saints, perhaps a folk memory of the hereditary guardians who once tended them.

falling into disuse. Eight hundred years after King Egbert's ruling, in 1686, the last Roman Catholic king of England, James II, went with his second wife to Holywell, Flint (Clwyd), where they partook of the waters of St Winefrid's well. This pilgrimage was undertaken with the hope of ensuring fertility and producing a son and heir for the uncertain monarch. Belief in the efficacy of wells was undiminished.

Sacred waters were best known for their therapeutic value. Certain chalybeate (iron-bearing) springs and fountains were often assigned curative powers. In ancient times these were centres of religious devotion, noted for the cure of specific illnesses. Perhaps the best attested examples can be found in Wales, which has a venerable tradition of holy wells dedicated to the numerous saints of that country. Nearly every well was at one time resorted to for the cure of various diseases or ailments, cures being effected either by drinking the waters or bathing in them. The holy well of St Gredifael, Ffynnon Redifael, was reputed to cure warts. Ffynnon Dydecho cured rheumatism, Ffynnon Wenog, (St Gwenog's well) cured young children with weak backs, but only if they were immersed in the well early in the morning before sunrise. Ffynnon Llechid was supposed to cure scrofula and kindred diseases, while St Teilo's well at Llandeilo was reputed to have the power to cure whooping cough. As at Ffynnon Wenog, special conditions had to be fulfilled if the cure was to prove successful: the sufferer had to drink the waters from Penglog Teilo, a cup made from a fragment of human skull, claimed to be that of St Teilo himself. The skull cup was only efficacious if administered to the patient by the eldest son of the tenant, an hereditary guardian.

Hereditary guardians of wells and other sacred shrines represented a Celtic tradition which persisted through a thousand years of Christianity, and the official title of such guardians, *doire*, has survived in the Scottish surname Dewar. These guardians are associated more with oracular than with curative powers, for just as the spirits of some wells could cure the sick, so those of others could predict the future. At Llanberis, next to St Peris's holy well (Ffynnon Beris), which was resorted to for the cure of rickets in children, there was a cottage under a rock known as Tynyffynnon where lived a hereditary wise woman whose task was to tend the two sacred trout kept in the well. The trout were the agents for oracular powers, which were interpreted by the wise woman, and visitors paid her for

Well-dressing at Tissington, Derbyshire. Though the designs date from the last century, the tradition goes back to time immemorial.

her services. Until the eighteenth century, when the tradition lapsed, St Gulval's well in Cornwall also had a resident wise woman who, for a payment, would take the waters and then make oracular pronouncements for the visitor.

Some prophetic wells did not need human intervention at all. The famous Drumming Well of Oundle 'drummed' when disaster was imminent. It is recorded by Baxter in *Certainty of the World of Spirits* (1691) that the Oundle well 'drummed' before the invasion of the Scottish army during the English Civil War, and again before the death of King Charles II. In Northamptonshire, Marvel Sike spring ran irregularly before a disaster, and St Helen's well at Rushton Spencer, Staffs., was said to dry up, no matter how wet the weather, when misfortune was due. In all these cases, the spirit of the well was held to be practising oracular powers, which could be for the benefit of humanity if correctly interpreted.

It was a universally observed custom to leave an offering for the spirit of the well in gratitude for the service it had rendered, and to ensure its continuance.

17

For personal favours, an offering of a piece of rag, a bent pin or a coin was generally sufficient. The superstition of throwing coins into wishing wells is a survival of this rite. In many places, in addition to personal offerings, the whole community decorated the local spring at the appropriate time of the year with flowers and branches. Although the designs now used are largely of Victorian origin and inspiration, the Derbyshire tradition of well-dressing is an authentic survival of this annual thanksgiving to the wells' spirits.

Other natural objects could participate in the well's sanctity. On Maelrubha, an island in Loch Maree, north Scotland, there was a small well in a special clearing, beside which stood 'the Tree', a bare, branchless, leafless trunk with unworked stones set around it. Both well and tree were said to be of great efficacy in the treatment of lunacy, and the latter was studded with coins, nails, screws and rusty fragments of iron, driven into it by visitors making wishes. In fact, belief in the efficacy of the tree outlived that of the well, whose powers were believed to have been destroyed in 1830, when a shepherd desecrated it by bringing a mad dog to be cured. The dog died the next day, the shepherd the following week. Before it finally ceased functioning, the well was also reputed to have oracular powers: Thomas Pennant in *A Tour in Scotland and Voyage to the Hebrides* (1772–4) noted, 'The visitants draw from the state of the well an omen of the disposition of St Maree: if his well is full they suppose he will be propitious; if not, they proceed in their operations with fears and doubts.'

Trees

Every tree is a living entity which, like other life, is born, grows to maturity, reproduces and dies. Permanently fixed to the earth at a specific place, the tree links earth and heaven and was formerly believed to be the residence of its peculiar spirit. Depending on the terrain, the role of trees in man's life differs. In arid conditions they serve to mark sources of water and provide shelter from the sun. In more temperate climates they form woodland and forests, as they did in the lowlands of Britain before the land was cleared for agricultural use. Today, hardly any virgin forest or woodland still exists in Britain. Even the New Forest and Epping Forest are only medieval replantings.

Trees often form prominent landmarks, and have been resorted to for various purposes since ancient

times. Until the last century, marriages were performed at an oak tree at Brampton, Cumbria, and the custom represented what was once a widespread practice, with so-called 'marriage oaks' existing in many places. It seems that these ceremonies were a christianization of much earlier fertility-promoting rites which had been performed at these trees or their forbears for many years. The usage was so persistent that Christianity could not extinguish it. It was enclosure of the commons and urbanization, not the zeal of missionaries, which finally dealt the death blow.

The tree's spirit was often invoked at meetings, both religious and secular, held in early times. Later, the prominence of the tree as a landmark, along with its traditional use as a meeting-place, ensured continuity. A tree might also provide the site for the administration of justice. The 'law trees' of medieval Germany, prominent limes, were the meeting-places of the secret vigilante Vehmic Courts, where supposed miscreants were tried. If the defendant's guilt was established, the tree served as a gallows. Near Thetford, Norfolk, the ancient tree called Ket's Oak still stands. During Ket's rebellion against King Edward VI in 1549, Ket's headquarters was at that tree, and his followers were encamped around it. Court was held at the oak, and justice meted out. Even today, in South Africa, the Pedi tribe has such a tree in the *letlatswa* (enclosed ground) of each *kgoro* (village), under which men gather for ritual ceremonies and the dispensation of justice.

Because of the sacred nature of these trees, it was considered a serious offence to injure or destroy one, sustained as it was by the spiritual powers of the place.

In ancient Irish law, the destruction of one of the seven holy Noble Trees (Apple, Alder, Birch, Hazel, Holly, Oak and Willow) was punishable by the fine of a cow, an extremely valuable property in a poor society. Even today such a holy tree, known as a 'skeog', is revered in country districts of Ireland, and remains untouched. This reverence for trees is worldwide. Only a few years ago, local workmen refused to fell a holy tree on the site of an extension to Singapore Airport. European workmen had to be called in to demolish it.

Numerous towns and places bear names which attest to the preeminent importance of such holy trees. Selly Oak, Birmingham, Goff's Oak, Herts, and Bracon Ash, Suffolk, are but three of hundreds of such names which can be found in every county. Most of the trees which have been thus immortalized were boundary-markers, like the celebrated Whiteleaved Oak, which stood at an important religious site at the junction of the former counties of Worcestershire, Gloucestershire and Herefordshire. This tree's site is part of a complex system of landscape geometry, which will be discussed in a later chapter (p. 80ff). In general the sites which preserve the names of holy trees are not those which were transformed in Christian times into the sites of churches. Although the churchyard yew tree is still commonplace in England, there exist few examples where trees superseded by churches were important enough to be remembered in place-names. The church of St Martin at Oak in Norwich recalls the previous existence of a pre-Christian sacred oak at the site, but this is one of the few churches so named. The survival of non-christianized sites as place-names is far more common. On the other hand, there are references in folklore to saints' staves being thrust into the ground and immediately putting forth leaves. This is recorded in the legends of Joseph of Arimathea at Wearyall Hill, Glastonbury, and of St Etheldreda at Etheldredestow, Norfolk, and the stories are no doubt folk memories of the deliberate planting of sacred trees to mark important geomantic places.

As the old trees died, new ones were planted in their place, continuing the mark-point. Only in recent times have they been allowed to die without replacement: hence the dead remnant of celebrated trees such as Merlin's Oak in Carmarthen. The prosperity of the town of Carmarthen, even its very survival, was in local lore held to depend upon the continued existence of this tree. The origin of this belief was a prophecy, attributed to Merlin:

When Myrddin's [Merlin's] tree shall tumble down
Then shall fall Carmarthen town.

Because of this legend, the tree, which was held to embody the spirit which sustained the town of Carmarthen, is still protected and supported by the local authorities. Formerly, it would have been replaced by a new tree from one of its acorns, but now it remains, a dead trunk, mute reminder of an all-but-dead tradition.

As we have seen, holy trees often had pins or nails driven into them to mark sacrifices. People would resort to special trees for the cure of various afflictions in exactly the same way that wells were visited, and there was sometimes a connection between the two, as on the island of Maelrubha in Loch Maree. In Belgium, at a crossroads between Eigenbrakkel and Le Feriet, stood two aged pine trees which had formerly flanked a cross (removed *c.* 1850). It was an ancient custom to insert pins or nails into the pines, or sometimes into the cross itself, in order to obtain a cure for fever. The cross was dedicated to St Etto, a seventh-century Irish missionary.

A tree in Vienna, the Stock-im-Eisen, had been driven so full of nails that it was completely covered with metal. From ancient times it had been traditional for every journeyman carpenter, joiner or mason who passed through the city to hammer a nail into this unfortunate tree.

The rite of hammering nails into trees appears to have been transferred to wooden effigies of gods and saints. Breton girls used to visit the shrine of St Guirec, which stood on a rock below the tideline at Perros Guirec, to pray for a husband, the fertility rite being concluded by the supplicant sticking a pin into a wooden effigy of the saint. West African fetishes are also often hammered full of nails, each nail representing a supplication.

Unworked stones
Rocks and stones have always held a special fascination for the human race, particularly the great outcrops, shaped into bizarre forms by millennia of weathering, which stand above the surrounding countryside in many places, forming major landmarks visible for miles around. The granite tors of Dartmoor, strangely shaped rock piles like the Cheesewring in Cornwall, and the Externsteine in Germany, bear the marks of this interest, from the carvings of the Stone Age to the

The sanctity of stone: top, the Externsteine rocks, a strange natural formation believed to be the geomantic centre of the German nation. Above, the Stone of Destiny, set beneath the Coronation Chair in Westminster Abbey, is still considered essential in the confirmation of the monarch as ruler.

graffiti of the twentieth century. These massive forms, visited since antiquity by travellers and pilgrims, seem to mark a place where the essence of the earth can still be perceived. Such places were regarded as habitations of the earth's spirit and, like holy hills, were visited in order to obtain states of heightened vision or enlightenment, and as ideal retreats for ascetics. 'Rock of Ages', the well-known Anglican hymn, was inspired by just such a rock, having been composed in the last century by the Reverend Toplady while he was sheltering from a rainstorm in the neighbourhood of Cheddar.

Outcrops like the Cheesewring are massive piles, large enough to climb upon. Far more common as objects of veneration are smaller, unworked stones, varying in size from ten-foot megaliths to boulders little larger than a football. The peculiar power discerned in certain of these stones has caused them to be revered since ancient times as sacred: Jacob's Pillow, for instance, the stone on which Jacob laid his head and received a vision which sanctified the place as Beth-El, the House of God. The word is cognate with the Greek *baitylos*, a type of meteoric stone which was relatively frequent in ancient Greece.

The Greek writer Pausanias mentions certain stones of this type which were kept in the temple of the Charities at Orchomenos in Boeotia. 'The stones are especially revered, and are said to have fallen from

The Omphalos of Delphi,
inscribed in archaic lettering with
the name of the earth goddess Ga,
was discovered in 1913 beneath
the inner sanctum of the temple.
This is the original baitylos
which was superseded by a more
elaborate carved omphalos.

heaven,' he wrote. He thought them notable in comparison with the 'statues made with art' of his own era, an indication of the stones' existence on that site *before* the temples in which they were kept.

Stones like these, which had fallen from heaven, now known as aerolites or meteorites, were especially valued, as they were believed to have come directly from the gods. Damascius, a Syrian writer of the sixth century of the Christian era, in his account of the life of Isidore, describes the baitylos of Elagabalus at Emesa in Syria:

I saw [he says] the baitylos moving through the air, at one time hidden in drapery, at another carried in the hands of the attendant, whose name was Eusebios. He said that there once came upon him the desire to wander at midnight far out of the city of Emesa to the mountain on which stands an ancient temple of Athena. There he sat down to rest from his journey; when all of a sudden he saw a ball of fire fall from on high, and a great lion standing beside it. And the lion straightway vanished; but he ran to the ball, the fire being extinguished, and found it to be the baitylos. He took it up and asked to which of the gods it belonged, and it said that it belonged to 'the Noble One' . . . When struck on the side it would give forth the answer sought for by the enquirer, uttering a thin shrill sound which Eusebios interpreted. . . . Indeed, I thought there was something divine in the baitylos, but Isidore said it was rather daemonic, for it was some daemon which made it move – not one of the more harmful ones, nor of the more material sort, not yet one of those which are raised up to the level of immortality, nor of the kind that is entirely pure.

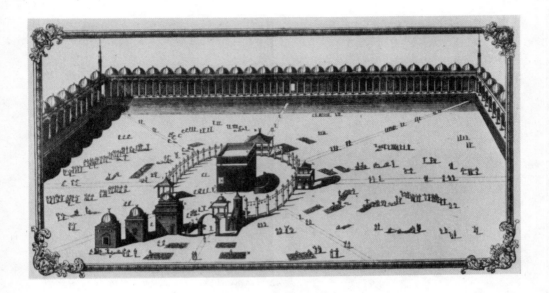

The Ka'aba at Mecca, disguised in its traditional black cube, is the centre of the Islamic world, acting as the focus for eight lines which radiate from it to the four cardinal points and the four corners of the globe.

The attributes of this baitylos are especially interesting, as in it are combined all the attributes commonly assigned to sacred stones. In addition to falling from the sky, it was found under special circumstances, it moved under its own will, it was kept in a special place, and it was an oracle, possessed by a spirit. Many British stones are often assigned one or more of these properties by local folklore, which remains a vast storehouse of more or less garbled geomantic knowledge. All over the world, stones have been said to move, heal, or pronounce – common properties which are universally recognized.

Several great religious shrines are based upon rocks or stones. The most holy shrine of Islam, the Ka'aba at Mecca, contains a stone which is believed to have fallen from the sky. The original Omphalos at Delphi, seat of the Oracle of Apollo, was a baitylos, daily anointed with oil. Many Christian churches were placed over such stones, or incorporated them in their actual fabric. The symbols of the ancient nature religion were not destroyed, but instead were often absorbed into the new religions which superseded the former cult. The earth energies perceived by the ancients to be manifested at or in these stones were thus refocused for the use of the new faith, the visible expression of the old being transformed into the visible expression of the new while retaining a memory of the new faith's victory over the old.

Hills

Ancient literature provides us with numerous instances of heroes or religious leaders ascending holy hills in order to communicate with the gods. Almost every religion on earth has its own holy mountain, and smaller local versions may be found in most districts. Since time immemorial, shrines have been placed on the top of hills. Such eminences have often been seen, like Mount Olympus, as the seat of the gods, holy mountains sacred to the male principle. Mounds, on the other hand, which are frequently artificial (e.g. the Neolithic Silbury Hill), or modifications of natural features, may be connected with aspects of nature – fertility, etc. – and thus embody the female principle.

In their natural state, holy hills are as unremarkable as any ordinary hill. The physical act of climbing a steep hill like Croagh Patrick or Glastonbury Tor is sufficient to cause a change in the physiological and psychological states of the climber. Heartbeat rate and depth of breathing increase to bring a greater amount of oxygen to the brain, producing a state of euphoria comparable with that achieved by breathing exercises. The change of scale of the world when viewed from the top, coupled with increased awareness, produces fresh insights into the nature of things.

In northern Europe, such holy hills, once sacred to the pagan religions, are often dedicated to St Michael, the christianized solar diety whose spear transfixes the earth current symbolized by the dragon, fusing earth and heaven at a fixed point. In Britain, Glastonbury Tor and St Michael's Mount, Cornwall, which both bear a church dedicated to St Michael, are the most spectacular of such holy hills. Both have a long pre-Christian history. Glastonbury Tor, whose sides appear to have been modified into a vast three-dimensional labyrinth, was the holy hill of the Celtic god of the underworld, Gwyn ap Nudd. Legend recounts its conversion to Christianity by St Collen who, summoned up the hill to the god's supernatural castle, dispersed the whole panoply of finery, courtiers and ceremony with a sprinkler full of holy water.

Mont St Michel, the French counterpart of St Michael's Mount, was known in pagan times as Dinsul, the holy Mount of the Sun. It was christianized in AD 710 by a mystic apparition of St Michael, the 'Vision of the Guarded Mount'. The abbey of St Michael's Mount in Cornwall was not founded until 1044. Believed to have originated inland (it was known in Cornish as Carrek Los en Cos, the Grey Rock in the Wood), the

Opposite, *hill churches
dedicated to St Michael, the
christianized solar deity:
above, Tor Hill, Glastonbury,
once sacred to the Celtic god of
the underworld; below, St
Michael's Mount, Cornwall,
with its eleventh-century
monastery. Both these holy
mountains are on the same 'St
Michael's Line'.*

mount was supposed to have been constructed by Cormoran and his wife, both giants. This is, perhaps, a folk memory of its partly artificial origin, since it was believed that hills in their natural state often needed modification to fulfil their function as gatherers of solar power. Numerous St Michael's hills, now crowned by churches or their remains, show evidence of shape modification for geomantic purposes. China affords countless examples of modification of hills' shapes in order that they might conform more fully to the principles of geomancy. Fortunately, Chinese geomancy, Feng-Shui, is amply documented, and, indeed, still practised in Chinese-occupied territories not under Communist rule. An extremely complicated set of rules and correspondences governs Feng-Shui, and analogies can be drawn with the ancient modifications of the British landscape which we can still see. In Feng-Shui, mountains correspond with the planets, their shape determining which planet, elements or attributes they possess. The Rev. J. Eitel, discussing the attributes of mountains in *Feng-Shui, or the Rudiments of Natural Science in China* (1873) wrote:

It is therefore one of the first requirements of a geomancer that he should be able to tell at a moment's glance which star is represented by any given mountain. As to the planets and their counterparts on earth, the rules by which each mountain may be referred to one or other of the five planets are very simple. If a peak rises up bold and straight, running out into a sharp point, it is identified with Mars and declared to represent the element fire. If the point of a similarly-shaped mountain is broken off and flat but comparatively narrow, it is said to be the embodiment of Jupiter and to represent the element wood. If the top of the mountain forms an extensive plateau, it is the representative of Saturn, and the element earth dwells there. If a mountain runs up high but its peak is softly rounded, it is called Venus and represents the element metal. A mountain whose top has the shape of a cupola is looked upon as the representative of Mercury, and the element water rules there.

A possible parallel may exist in Britain. Solar hills dedicated to St Michael were generally crowned with a church, and other hills can be found dedicated to quite different saints, which may well also be christianizations of former gods. In practice many hills were used for beacons, sacred bonfires lit at Beltane and other festivals of the year. Numerous hills are known by the name 'beacon' in testimony of their erstwhile function – Dunkery Beacon, the Brecon Beacons, Herefordshire Beacon, etc. These were also used for signalling purposes from ancient times until the eighteenth

A place of modern pilgrimage, Croagh Patrick (St Patrick's holy mountain), in County Mayo, Eire, recalls the ancient and pre-Christian ritual perambulation.

century, when they were superseded by semaphore telegraphy. Several beacon hills are dedicated to St Anne. These were formerly hills holy to Santan, a fire god with a name linguistically cognate with the modern Welsh word *tan*, fire. Whether fire hills are different in form from St Michael's (sun) hills has not yet been fully investigated.

The St Michael's hills at Glastonbury and Burrowbridge Mump both have traces of labyrinths. The path to the top of the sacred hill may often be indirect, as at Glastonbury Tor, or may provide a painful barefoot pilgrimage, such as the annual ceremonial walk up Croagh Patrick, St Patrick's holy hill in Ireland, where the popular custom still flourishes. Ascent of these hills on the correct day by the prescribed route was (and is) held to be of spiritual benefit to the pilgrim.

The calendar and standing stones

The sun, without which the earth itself would of course not exist, sustains all life upon this planet. Its periodicity controls the unique biological cycles innate in living organisms, since day and night, summer and winter, are directly related to the earth's position to the sun. To the earliest men, integrated with these natural cycles, the chief measure of time must have been sunrise and sunset, though naturally the moon's recurrent phases were also of great importance in determining longer periodicities. In the higher latitudes, recolonized at the end of the last Ice Age, it was evident that the seasons of growth and decline could be measured in relation to day length, the period of the sun.

The simplest form of time measure, in common usage until recently, was and is that of the gnomon. Consisting simply of a stick thrust into the ground, the gnomon casts a shadow whose length and position indicate the time of the day, the season of the year and, given a reliable calibration, the latitude of the gnomon itself. The gnomon may have been the first scientific instrument, and it has since proved capable of almost infinite improvement and refinement.

It must soon have been realized that the height of the gnomon determined the length of the shadow and time of day, the length varying according to the time of year and hence a measurement of the seasonal variations. This realization may have led to the earliest standardization of measures, as standardizing a gnomon against a dial made with a gnomon of standard length could be readily achieved. The imperial measures of ancient China were determined according to a standard gnomon, directly relating to time and, because the gnomon had to be at a specific latitude, to place. Lengths of shadow from gnomons of known height at known latitude were used by the Greek geometer Eratosthenes to measure the circumference of the earth, and similar attempts were made in ancient China.

With the invention of agriculture, determination of planting and harvest times became a matter of the utmost importance. Originally related to lunar cycles, this was gradually formalized into a calendar, which with continuing observations was progressively refined. The fundamental record of the seasons and the increase and decline in the length of day in relation to the calendar was necessarily a complex task which could not be undertaken by the untutored, and this inevitably led to the rise of the specialist. Science, magic and religion were an integrated discipline in ancient times, simply forming divergent aspects of the same corpus of applied knowledge. Specialists in astronomical observation were thus also members of the priesthood, guardians of all knowledge concerning the apparent paths of the major luminaries and their use in compiling calendars, astrological prediction and divination.

In effect, this observation was the beginning of a technology of control: a precise science as opposed to

Winter sunset at Stonehenge, where the configuration marks each important solstitial and equinoctial event.

the spontaneity inherent in nature religion. In order to transmit the knowledge, a formal apparatus was introduced – the beginnings of organized religion.

Of course, observations of the heavenly bodies had taken place since the nomadic period. They had always been used for navigation on land and sea, but precise measurement and record of astronomical phenomena were not possible unless the observer had an observatory – a fixed place where the annual and long-term variations of the heavens would be gauged in relation to unchanging landmarks.

At first, the observations were of the most basic kind. Viewing the sunrise and sunset each day from a marked place, the observer noted each position in relation to the horizon's mark-points, hills or mountains. The primitive astronomer was able to determine the halfway point between the extreme rise and set positions by observation, perhaps marking the line with a stick if the horizon did not have a suitable natural marker at that orientation. When sunrise and sunset were on this line, it was noted that day and night were the same length – the equinoxes. As knowledge of the sun's apparent behaviour grew more precise, further markers would have been required.

At this point we go beyond the essential observations and records required by the necessity for a permanent calendar. The more precise the observations, the more inaccurate they were shown to be, owing to the complex factors of refraction and occasional standstills in sunset over several days.

More and more complex astronomical observations were devised to study, record and predict these phenomena. Great systems of poles for sighting the rising and the setting of sun and moon were erected and taken down as, over the years, additional aspects of their complicated paths were determined.

Once these positions had been finalized, they were marked permanently by setting up large stones in precisely the correct position – with an accuracy which has survived to the present.

Finally, highly complex structures like Avebury, Carnac, Callanish and Stonehenge were erected. Cunningly designed to incorporate several functions, their true nature has only recently been rediscovered.

Megalithic structures indicated the positions of the solstices and equinoxes, which could be used for checking the accuracy of the calendar. They also embodied the information required for the determination of irregular events, such as long-term cycles of the sun and moon, their perturbations and eclipses. Apart from the necessity of monitoring the seasons so that agriculture might proceed properly, and religious festivals might be held on the correct days, the accurate prediction of eclipses was required so that the appropriate magical precautions could be taken against their malevolent influence. The unusual behaviour patterns of animals during total eclipses of the sun are well known. Birds stop singing and an eerie silence descends upon the land. The earth's magnetic field and

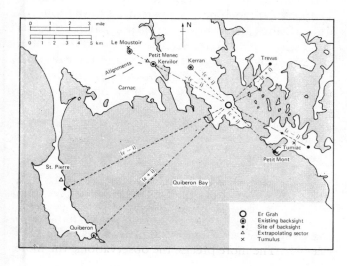

The skilled work of ancient geomancers has been decoded by Professor Thom at Er Grah, Brittany, a 67-foot-high, 340-ton megalith which was transported to this precise spot and erected to serve as a 'universal lunar foresight' marking the extreme positions of the moon during its 18.6-year cycle.

solar radiation are also interrupted when an eclipse takes place, as radio and television technicians know to their cost. The dowsable currents of the earth, which have been found to alter according to the phases of the moon, are affected by lunar eclipses. Any geomantic functions which required divinatory methods could not be carried out on such days, knowledge which would be useful to have in advance.

To this end, complex astronomically orientated structures were constructed all over the planet, combining a religious with an observational and record-keeping function. Of such observatories, which were constructed by many ancient civilizations, Stonehenge on Salisbury Plain in England is the most celebrated and probably the most studied.

For centuries it has been known that sunrise on midsummer day can be viewed from the centre of the circle over the Heelstone along the approach avenue. Since time immemorial, until the government erected barbed wire and charged admission, local inhabitants used to gather to observe the Midsummer sunrise, perhaps in unbroken and authentic continuity from ancient times.

The work of many researchers over the past century has shown that numerous astronomical functions can be assigned to Stonehenge, including its use as a computer for determining the dates of lunar eclipses. One of the most interesting facts to emerge from this welter of research is that Stonehenge is uniquely fitted to its place and its function.

As we see it today, Stonehenge is an enigmatic ruin, popularly supposed to be the site of hideous Druidic sacrifices and obscure astronomical observations. Since the time of Inigo Jones, chief architect to the court of King Charles I, scores of antiquaries, archaeologists and astronomers have examined, mused over and speculated about the ancient stones and their original function. Only in this century, however, have plausible analyses been made of the stones' position in relation to astronomical phenomena.

The importance of Stonehenge in ancient times is attested in references from classical authors. Diodorus Siculus, for instance, wrote in *c.* 50 BC:

The moon when viewed from this island appears to be but a little distance from the earth. . . . The account is given also that the god visits the island every 19 years, the period in which the return of the stars to the same place in the heavens is accomplished. . . . There is also in the island both a magnificent sacred fane of Apollo, and a notable temple. . . .

This reference may be taken to refer to Stonehenge as an observatory of both sun (Apollo) and moon (the 19-year cycle of 'the god'), including their relative cycles of motion in relation to the stars. That such information should be known to Diodorus in the Mediterranean is strong evidence of the importance of Stonehenge even at such a late date as 50 BC. Geoffrey of Monmouth, writing in the twelfth century AD, recounted a legend that the stones had been transported to their present site from Ireland, 'not by force, but by Merlin's art'. Merlin, according to Geoffrey the wizard mentor of the British king Aurelius Ambrosius, was called in to move the Giant's Dance (an alternative name for Stonehenge) from Ireland, when ordinary muscle power had proved ineffectual. This legend, like Diodorus's 'nineteen years', was dismissed as a fable or an imaginative embellishment until modern petrological analysis proved that the bluestones at Stonehenge were not of local origin, but had indeed been transported from the west, as recorded in Monmouth's *History of the Kings of Britain*. Their origin was not Ireland, however, but Mynydd Preseli (the Preseli Mountains) in Wales. The transport of these stones was a feat quite exceptional for the period, and if the mind behind it was the 'Merlin' of Monmouth, he must have been a remarkable genius.

Many surveys, more or less accurate, have been made of Stonehenge, and it was only a matter of time until each and every part of this remarkable edifice was accounted for. Excavation has demonstrated that Stonehenge is not a construction erected at a single time, but the accretions of centuries: building, demolition, redesign and reconstruction as knowledge and techniques were refined. Stonehenge has had three major stages, all of which fit into an overall pattern, culminating in the famous circle of trilithons which remain in ruined form today.

Many researchers, noting the local tradition according to which local inhabitants formerly resorted to Stonehenge on Midsummer Day to greet the sunrise, have attempted to unravel the solar mysteries preserved in the stones' siting. But only in recent years has a coherent picture begun to emerge. In 1963 Gerald Hawkins, professor of astronomy at Boston (Massachusetts) University, published a paper in the respected scientific journal *Nature* which suggested that the twelve major alignments of sunrise and moonrise, eight lunar and four solar, were delineated by the relative positions of the Stonehenge stones. The next year he announced his discovery that the 56 'Aubrey holes', the excavated remains of one of the earlier circles on the site, could have been used in the prediction of lunar eclipses, as their number was related to the 18.6-year cycle of the moon alluded to by Diodorus Siculus. In 1965 the celebrated book *Stonehenge Decoded* was finally published, which gathered together and evaluated his previous discoveries.

Among other fascinating facts concerning the geometry of the stones' positions, Hawkins showed that Stonehenge could not function elsewhere without alteration being made to its geometry. For instance, the only place where the four 'station stones' which determine lunar and solar alignments would form an exact rectangle is at the latitude of Stonehenge. Move it but a few miles to the north or south, and the geometry would no longer be functional. This fact makes the concrete replica of Stonehenge in Washington State, USA, an astronomically useless folly.

Although it is undoubtedly the best known stone circle in the world, Stonehenge is far from unique in possessing a complex astronomically orientated geometry. Dr Alexander Thom, former professor of engineering science at Oxford University, by his painstaking surveys of over 500 megalithic structures in Britain and Brittany, established that they too were laid out with precise geometry, incorporating fixed measures. From his statistical analyses of stone circles, expounded in his books *Megalithic Sites in Britain* and *Megalithic Lunar Observatories*, he discovered a constant unit, termed by him the Megalithic Yard (MY) of 2.72 feet. This Megalithic Yard has been found to have been used in multiples and sub-multiples in the geometry of stone circles and alignments in Scotland, Wales, England and Brittany, and Thom has backed up his discoveries with impressive statistical evidence. Some metrologists have noted that the relation between the English foot and the Megalithic Yard (1:2.72) is the same as the ratio of unity to the base of natural logarithms, e, pointing to some ancient but now forgotten connection between the two seemingly disparate units.

Thom's most important discovery, in geomantic terms, demonstrates the subtlety with which geometry was used by the ancients. His work shows that their geometrical systems were often based upon a figure first recorded by Pythagoras, namely, the triangle with a right-angle and sides of integral length, from which is derived the famous theorem: the square on the

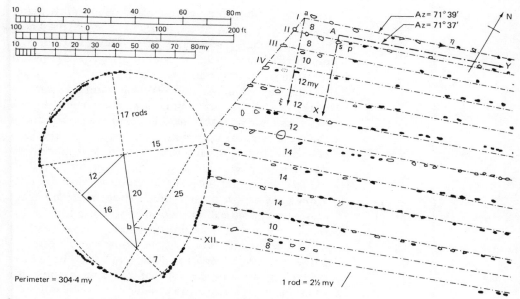

Perimeter = 304·4 my

1 rod = 2½ my

hypotenuse of a right-angled triangle is equal to the sum of the squares of the other two sides. Thus the triangles produced by the measurements (in MY) 3, 4, 5; 5, 12, 13; 8, 15, 17; 12, 35, 37; and 9, 40, 41 have been found to form the basic geometry underlying the patterns of very many stone circles.

Circles they may be called, but ever since the work of the earliest antiquarian pioneers it has been well known that they are not true circles. This was often put down to the supposed incompetence of the builders. Thom's researches showed that the megalithic geometricians, far from being inaccurate, were precision engineers, preferring to use whole-number multiples of the Megalithic Yard in their designs, presumably for unknown mystical reasons. The 'circles' which are not circular, but elliptical, ovoid or irregular, have been shown by Thom to be the result of a concrete application of a hitherto lost geometrical system, derived logically from 'Pythagorean' triangles laid out many centuries before Pythagoras himself was born.

Avebury, whose position is determined by the overall landscape geometry of the area, was laid out from a 3, 4, 5 triangle with units of 25 MY, so that all derived dimensions come out in multiples of 5 or 10. Not only do these sites demonstrate a phenomenally accurate method of survey and design, but a large proportion of them were designed to function as sophisticated solar and lunar observatories. Use of the standard measure – the Megalithic Yard – which was the essential connecting link between the whole

Thom's survey of the end of the Carnac (Brittany) alignments demonstrates the megalithic engineers' precise concern with Pythagorean geometry hundreds of years before Pythagoras was born.

complex of sites, has been detected in megalithic sites up to 1,000 miles apart, perhaps one of the most significant facts to emerge from Thom's studies. It points to the setting and maintaining of a fixed constant measure which was perhaps manufactured in one place and distributed, in the same way that standard measures of the present day are maintained. The possession of a fixed system of measurement is as much a precondition for the existence of civilization over a large area as a common language. Countless systems have since been devised, or have superseded former systems. But to enforce a constant measure, a certain level of organization and purpose must exist. Even if the arrangement was not a political or national organization in the modern sense, it would have existed as a coherent system within the body of practitioners. The knowledge and application of the constant would have been preserved, as was the lore of the Freemasons, for example, in esoteric form available only to the initiated, and hence it was lost with the collapse of the social system which sustained them.

Fixing the place

2

So far we have considered natural sites only, where the energies of the place had merely to be discovered, not 'fixed' by human agency. But sites where there were no obvious visible landmarks or features, such as springs, rocky outcrops or trees, had to be marked out by other means.

The most direct way of divining sites of energy was by means of the rod. Dowsing, often called 'water divining', is an art which can be traced back into the distant past. Dowsers can detect alterations in underground conditions indicating waterlines, metal objects, etc., and their services are still in demand today. Moses is recorded as having used a rod to discover water, and the solar deity Mithras divined water with a bow and arrow. In addition to their well-known ability to detect underground water and metal, dowsers find their rods responding to other kinds of properties or lines of energy, sometimes called 'geodetic', and these qualities have often been noted by dowsers at megalithic sites like Stonehenge. Such features as boundary stones, ancient roads and tracks, as well as ecclesiastical buildings (themselves on pre-Christian sites), have been shown to be marked by special geodetic patterns. In his book *The Pattern of the Past* Guy Underwood suggested, on the basis of his dowsing fieldwork, that certain individual features of church buildings are marked by their own peculiar characteristics. For instance, north and south doors and porches were found to be set upon transverse lines, naves and chancels upon geodetic lines, and high altars were marked by spirals. Whether all these phenomena were present before the building was erected, or were modified by the presence of the building, is still a controversial subject. What is certain is that they reveal to the dowser a discernible special pattern which was there before the edifice was constructed, the pattern having been previously identified by some agency – a geomancer, a priest, a member of the arcane brotherhood, a 'wise' man or woman, or even an animal.

These patterns can be perceived by animals and people with powers of dowsing. The forces thus

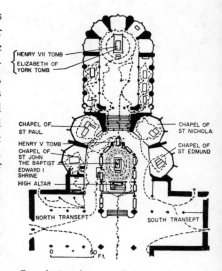

Correlations between shrines and underground energy lines are seen in the patterns dowsed by Guy Underwood at the east end of Westminster Abbey. The shrine of King Edward the Confessor, for centuries an important place of pilgrimage, is seen to be located over an especially powerful 'blind spring'.

This mummified cat was found walled up in a mill at Sudbury, Suffolk, probably as a sacrifice to a malevolent influence. Its removal was followed by the collapse of the roof at that precise spot. The practice of sacrificial foundations still continues in many countries.

identified were therefore deliberately channelled for a specific purpose. The attributes of these special places were thus captured, enhanced and guided into the service of mankind by the geomantic construction, the creation of special physical, psychological and spiritual states attainable only with difficulty elsewhere. The site, invested with a natural aura, was enclosed, its forces disciplined for a specific purpose rather than allowed to seep away into the external continuum. Use of the divining rod enabled others to verify the findings of the original diviner, a useful faculty in the case of secular boundary disputes, and essential to the rediscovery of the sites of lost buildings where only an approximate location was known.

It is probable, for example, that the site for the refounding of St Albans Abbey was discovered with the use of the rod. Time and again, legend recounts the reconsecration of old, forgotten, obliterated sites, with guardian angels appearing to some devout person.

There are many cases, recorded and legendary, of geomantic divination of sacred sites by animals in Britain and elsewhere. Underwood noted that cows and other animals prefer certain places in fields, these sites being detected as active sites by dowsers, and known as 'blind springs' (i.e. places where changes in the water level have probably taken place). In parts of Africa and North America, it was the practice to sew together the eyelids of a creature and let it wander at will until it lay down, the place where it stopped being divined as 'the place'. The monks of Holy Island, seeking a site for a shrine for St Cuthbert, were shown the site at Dunholm by a dun cow. There they founded a monastery which later became Durham Cathedral, a building incorporating a carving of its founder – the Dun Cow of Durham. The event is also commemorated in the name of Dun Cow Lane, next to the Cathedral close.

Waltham, another major English abbey, also had its site divined by animal agency, but in an unusual way, suggesting that the sanctity of one site could be deliberately transferred to another. On the top of St Michael's Hill at Montacute in Somerset, a buried flint crucifix was discovered, having been revealed to a man in a dream. The crucifix was placed in a cart pulled by a team of eight oxen, which were permitted to make their own way across country until they would go no further. At that point, Waltham Abbey was founded, with the crucifix its most valued relic.

Animals' skulls were frequently found as sacrificial offerings in the foundations of old houses and churches.

In the case of very early constructions, it is probable that the skulls and bones belonged to an animal which was allowed to wander at will in order to divine the site. It would have been sacrificed on the spot, defining the act of foundation in time and place. The animal's spirit, by means of its untimely demise, was fixed in the place, and acted as a supernatural guardian of the building against malevolent intrusion.

In East Anglia, the remains of cats, mummified by being placed in attics where they were dehydrated by smoke, have been found in the roofs of a number of buildings. These animals were certainly placed there in order to protect the building, and may have been utilized in the divination of the site of the house.

In 1975 one was found in a mill at Sudbury in Suffolk, and was removed, as the mill was undergoing reconstruction for conversion into a hotel. Numerous inexplicable fires and disasters attended its subsequent travels, and the roof collapsed in the old mill at the place where the cat had been found, causing £60,000 worth of damage. The cat was then immediately brought back, and reburied in its original grave, along with a note apologizing for the disturbance. It appears in this case that the cat was placed at a specific place in order to nullify a malevolent influence at that point, for, since the cat's reburial, there have been no more disastrous occurrences.

Tombs

Burial places, especially those of famous men, have always been revered. Where the body lay, something of the person's spirit was believed to reside, imbuing the place with a special sanctity.

The various kinds of burial mounds – round barrows, long barrows, bell barrows – which are encountered all over northern Europe, despite millennia of wholesale destruction, are near-permanent memorials of the dead who lie within. Guy Underwood detected at least one blind spring beneath each long barrow he dowsed. The majority had a blind spring in the middle of the highest part of the barrow. Important dead were buried in places where their residual spiritual energy would integrate with the spirit of the earth.

Two or three thousand years later, in the Roman period and the early Middle Ages, it was customary to erect the 'martyrium', a temple or church built around the remains of the saint, king or hero, on the site of burial, or else to 'translate' the body to a new shrine. Thousands of such places exist all over Europe, along

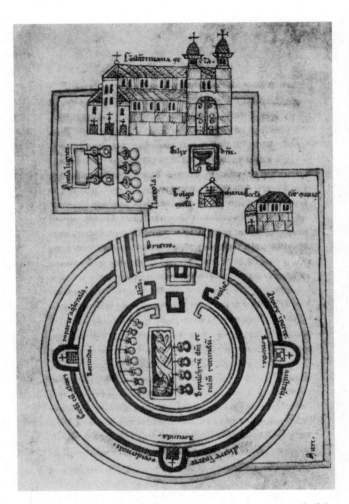

The archetypal Christian martyrium: an early thirteenth-century plan of the Holy Sepulchre, Jerusalem.

with their reputed miracles and cures, probably representing sites of earth power known for millennia whose sanctity was appropriated, and perhaps reinforced, by becoming the burial places of the holy.

The archetypal Christian martyrium was the Holy Sepulchre church in Jerusalem, which was traditionally founded by the empress Helena, on the site of the tomb of Christ. Helena was the mother of the emperor Constantine, who established Christianity as the official religion of the Roman empire. This church, the pattern for numerous later European edifices, was circular, being supposedly the centre of the world, the place of Christ's sepulchre occupying the exact centre. For centuries this site was revered as the Holy of Holies of Christendom, so much so that the Saracen Caliph al-Hakim had it demolished in AD 1009, in order to keep its influence from tainting Islam. It was reconstructed, however, when the Christians recaptured Jerusalem, on the orders of Constantine Monomach in 1048.

The Venerable Bede, earliest English (rather than British) historian, mentions a number of miraculous events associated with soil from the death place of King Oswald of Northumbria, killed at the battle of Maserfeld, AD 641. The earth had effective healing properties, he reported, and even the power miraculously to extinguish fire. However, that particular site was only designated as that of the king's death *because* it had miraculous powers, the true site having been most probably forgotten during the rout of the Northumbrian army. It is therefore likely that a sacred area already existed at Maserfaeld which was appropriated by the disciples of the now canonized Oswald.

The earliest recorded Christian martyr in Britain was St Alban, executed by the Roman authorities at Verulamium at an unknown date during the Roman period. The site of his martyrdom was known from supposed contemporary accounts, and a church was erected there to commemorate the event. In time the church fell into disrepair, and disintegrated until it became indistinguishable from the other ruins of the once great Roman city. However, its position was re-divined by King Offa (or his geomancers) when he endowed the new abbey of St Albans, which, it was believed, had power as one of the key geomantic sites in England owing to its vital Christian importance.

Occasionally, epoch-making events like battles have been commemorated by the founding of sacred buildings in place of the more customary memorials. In Sussex, Battle Abbey was set up by William of Normandy to celebrate his triumph at Senlac over King

The feretory containing the relics of the protomartyr Alban, which were discovered by King Offa in a vision. Once found, they became the sanctifiers of St Albans Abbey, AD 795.

St Albans Cathedral, a Norman and later medieval rebuild of the foremost martyrium in England.

Harold II and the Saxon nation. Dedicated to St Martin, the abbey was endowed with all the land in a three-mile circle, encompassing six manors and three churches, making the abbey, and thus the battle's site, into the geomantic centre of the area. It is even possible that the choice of site for the battle was influenced by geomancers, since kings were usually attended by a corps of magicians, astrologers, soothsayers and the like.

Continuity

The powers inherent in sacred sites have been used over the years by practitioners of many different creeds, and shrines of one religion have frequently been converted into the service of another. In a letter to the Abbot Mellitus on his mission to England, AD 604, Pope Gregory wrote:

I have determined, after mature deliberation on English affairs, that the temples of the idols of that nation ought by no means to be destroyed. Rather, let the idols that are in them be destroyed; let water be blessed and sprinkled in these temples; let altars be erected and relics placed in them. Provided the temples are well built, it is requisite that they should be converted from the worship of devils to the service of the True God.

In this way, the site's continuity was guaranteed. Christianization of such famous temples as the Parthenon in Athens, the temples of Isis at Philae in Egypt, and the Pantheon in Rome, are celebrated instances of this practice: so is the conversion of the great cathedral of Santa Sophia in Constantinople into a mosque. Of the many churches in England on pre-Christian foundations, those at Knowlton in Dorset, Mapelscombe in Kent, St Mabyn's in Cornwall, and Chesham in Buckinghamshire, are associated with ancient earthworks or standing stones. Churches at Taplow in Berkshire, Thriplow in Cambridge, and Ludlow in Shropshire, are built on pagan burial mounds.

Even as late as the last century, Christian missionaries in Madagascar were founding churches on the sites of pagan sacred stones where Christians had been martyred on the orders of Queen Rànavàlona. Six years later, they obtained the sites from the Christian king Radamas II, and constructed churches there. The mother church of Madagascar was set up at Ambàtonakànga, the Stone of the Guinea Fowl, which stood at the intersection of the two main roads of the capital, a place which represents the omphalos, or geomantic centre, in all cultures. The second church was erected on the sacred White Hill at Ambôhipòtsy, another at the Stone of Hurling, Ampàmarìna. Thus instead of abandoning the sacred sites, they were incorporated into the new religion, along with whatever powers they held. Madagascar had a powerful and complex tradition of geomancy and divination, with oracles, astrology and spiritism, so the destruction of the old shrines (but not abandonment of the sites) was a prerequisite for the introduction of the new.

Continuity of function is illustrated in the case of Hagia Sophia, the Byzantine emperor Justinian's Christian masterpiece which was converted into a mosque after the fall of Constantinople, 1453.

3

The omphalos

The celebrated Omphalos of Delphi, centre of the Greek world, marked the fixing of the earth spirit by the solar deity Apollo.

The concept of the centre of the world, the world's foundation stone, has occurred in different cultures all over the globe. To the individual, the place where he or she is at any given time is 'the place', a point from which the observed world is seen to originate. As the individual's spirit is centralized in the body, and the body has a physical location, so the world's spirit was thought of as centralized at a fixed point.

This point acted as the centre, a pivot about which everything else revolved. It remained fixed when all else moved, stable in both the whirling of the heavens in its cycles of days and years, and during earthquakes.

The fixation to a central place of the hitherto free energies of the earth, which were formerly able to wander almost at random, represents the change from the diffuse, worldwide shrine of the Earth Mother to the centralized, geomantically defined temple of the solar god. This changeover was long and drawn out. Coinciding with the beginning of urbanization, it marked the departure of at least part of mankind from direct communion with the earth. By means of this new-found power, the energizing spirit of the place which may usually have visited it perhaps once a year, was made fixed and accessible at all times. Once stabilized, the surroundings were modified in order to enhance the properties of the site, and an ever-increasing complexity of temple was added to utilize it to the utmost.

The word 'omphalos', meaning 'navel', is now generally applied to any divined geomantic centre. Originally, it referred to the Omphalos at Delphi, seat of the oracle of Apollo and centre of the Greek world. In legend, the site was divined by Zeus, who sent out two eagles (or swans) in order to determine the earth's true centre. One bird was released to the west, the other to the east. Where their paths crossed, at Delphi, the omphalos was defined. The stone which originally represented the omphalos had evidently been recognized as sacred from an early period, being an unworked stone or baitylos, symbol of the deity.

According to Strabo, the legend of Zeus was made tangible in the form of two gold eagles which were attached to the sides of the Omphalos, which by his time was an elliptical stone carved with a network pattern.

The Delphic Omphalos stone is found in numerous representations on Greek coins and vases. The network pattern was also carved on other stones which marked important geomantic sites. It has been found on elliptical Celtic markstones from Ireland and Germany, and may be seen in the interlaced patterns on Pictish, Celtic and Saxon standing stone crosses. The patterns symbolized the harnessing of the sites' energies, powers known universally as the serpent power. In later times these Saxon and Norse interlaced patterns were often shown explicitly with dragons' heads.

A Celtic omphalos, the Turoe Stone of County Galway, Eire, shares with its Delphic equivalent a 'binding' tracery of filigree pattern.

The Roman author Varro compared the Omphalos's shape with a 'treasury', the name commonly applied to primitive domed graves (such as the 'Treasury of Atreus' at Mycenae, so described by Pausanias). Since it was on the site of the old oracle of the earth goddess herself, this analogy is apt. For beneath the Omphalos, legend said that there lay buried Python, the serpent spirit of the earth, which had been killed by Apollo, the sun god. Seated on the Omphalos, Apollo thus sat upon the grave of his predecessor. The earth's energy, formerly free and apparent at the site only once a year, was fixed by the adherents of the cult of Apollo when the nature religion of the Earth Mother was overthrown. In common with Greece, many other cultures attributed this energy to the serpent or world dragon. This energy, rampant and untamed, was fixed when the omphalos was defined, i.e. at the moment when the spike or peg marking the spot was thrust into the ground during the foundation ceremony. In geodetic terms, a wandering blind spring of exceptional power was caused to stay permanently in the same place by the peg. In all omphalos legends, the emphasis is on the imposition of order on chaos, fixing the untamed and previously fickle serpent powers at a special point. From this point the energies could be tapped and channelled for the benefit of mankind.

In mythology, the fixing of this energy was depicted as a mortal struggle, not lightly undertaken, whose outcome was uncertain, puny man pitted against the massive forces of the earth. The enactment of this mortal encounter survives today in the Western legends of St George, Beowulf, Siegfried, St Martha, St Michael and countless benevolent giants. Symbolically, the

The earth dragon's head is pierced by a bishop's crozier, symbolizing the fixation of the earth's energies. From the font at Avebury, Wilts.

solar hero transfixes the dragon with his arrow, spear or lance. The sword of St Michael, the lance of St George or the arrows of giants like the Hertfordshire dragon-killer Piers Shonkes, all represent the peg or pole which pierced the dragon's head, immovably fixing it at the omphalos. Thus the powers of the sun and earth were fused at a specific place and time, potently defining the site.

Because of the nature of this power, the time of fixation had to be chosen with the utmost care; any error might bring ill fortune, which has traditionally attended those who have tampered with ancient geomantic works.

Being a place of exceptional energy, such a site was a link point between the earthly and celestial. For this reason, the omphalos was invariably protected from misuse by being covered with a stone, a shrine, or some other structure which denied access to the uninitiated. Such access was thus restricted to those who had the knowledge and spiritual maturity not to misuse the potent forces at their disposal.

The serpentine nature of such earth power was recognized all over the world. The oracle of Madagascar, Ramáhavály (the One Able to Answer), like the Delphic oracle, the lord and patron of serpents, was kept in a sacred cave on the holy mountain at Andringitra. Japanese tradition asserts that the earth was carried on a leviathan, Hishin-Uwo, which caused earthquakes when it moved. Such earthquakes were then quelled by a god who pinned down the errant power by means of the rivet-rock of the world, the Kaus-mi-ishi in Hitachi Province. The omphalos at

Delhi in India is marked by a great iron pillar, set up in the fourth century of the Christian era. Eight centuries later, the major mosque of that city was built around it, the new religion acquiring its sanctity. In tradition, this iron pillar was said to have been driven so deeply into the earth that it rested upon the head of Vasuki, the serpent king who supports the world. It was consequently known as the immovable sustainer of the kingdom.

In Norse mythology, the serpent power in the form of Nidhoggr, the earth serpent, continuously gnawed away at the roots of the great world-ash tree, Yggdrasill, indicating a belief that the serpent power, though pinned down on the omphalos, was slowly freeing itself. Frequent rededications were required to stabilize it; hence the legends of trapped giants, wolves or dragons, even the Devil, freeing themselves only to be hunted down by the gods.

A constant attribute of the omphalos was its immobility, its permanence, as it was seen not only as a point on the earth's surface, but as a link point between the earthly and the heavenly. On Yggdrasill as the cosmological omphalos, the German geomancer and regional planner Josef Heinsch commented:

The world serpent engraved on a Swedish stone, and containing in its body a runic message. The cross proclaims it as Christian in intent if not in content.

The Nordic cosmic tree Yggdrasill represents the axis linking the three planes of existence: Asgard, Midgard and Utgard.

A Chinese version (AD 168) of the universe-tree offers a close parallel with the Nordic Yggdrasill.

As the 'tree of measure', the world-axis of the ancients was more than an imaginary line in the universe, more than a conceptual extension of the point into the first dimension; it was not only the axis of rotation about which turn the outwardly visible stars of heaven, but the point of growth and origin of all appearing life in the polar images of microcosm and macrocosm, which were thought of according to a still basically flat or two-dimensional scheme, and represented on three different planes: the bright, divine, spiritual upperworld (Asgard): the earthly, corporeal middleworld (Midgard): and the dark, demonic, ghostly underworld (Utgard).

Here, the omphalos is seen as the point extended into new dimensions, linking the ternary of substance, nature and essence, a place on the earth's surface where other states may be reached.

Whenever it was set up, this omphalos was outwardly marked by a stone, a pillar, a pole or a tree. Being a link between the earth and the heavens, its precincts afforded protection, literally a sanctuary, as no violence could be done on the site without profaning this most holy place. In medieval Europe, such a sanctuary or moratorium on feudal violence was recognized when a fair was declared, by setting up a pole on the local omphalos, usually in the market-place: just as, in early times, the Delphic oracle was said to be active once a year, so, when the time was right, the local counterpart was set up. 'No feud could be prosecuted on the place whereto people came to trade, nor within a certain radius from it. . . . A stranger who came to trade was a guest, and he went under this very name. Even

Irminsul, the Saxon omphalos-pole, was cut down on the orders of the Christian emperor Charlemagne. In this carving from the Externsteine rocks, W. Germany, it acts as a stool for an attendant removing the body of Christ from the cross which now supersedes it.

the lord who had no scruples about robbing a merchant on the high road, respected the Weichbild, that is the pole which stood in the market-place and bore the king's arms, or a glove, or the image of a local saint, or a simple cross . . .' wrote Peter Kropotkin, in *Mutual Aid*. The Exeter Lammas Fair, the Barnstaple September Fair, and the Honiton Fair all preserve the raising of the glove, the Town Crier holding up a gilt glove on a decorative pole, crying 'Oyez, oyez, oyez, the glove is up!'

Knowledge of the position of an omphalos was of utmost importance. The utilization of the power ensured the continuance of a kingdom; its loss, the downfall of a nation. Charlemagne demonstrated the permanent nature of his Christian conquest of the pagan Saxons by cutting down their sacred omphalos-pole, the Irminsul.

The sanctity of the central point was later transferred to the stone which had for many years imbibed the powers of the omphalos. One such stone is the so-called Stone of Destiny, which now resides in a special niche in the Coronation Chair at Westminster Abbey. It originated in Ireland, being the royal omphalos stone upon which successive kings of Ireland were crowned. As such it was kept at the correct place, so that at the moment of coronation, divined by the astrologers, all the auspicious conditions would be fulfilled – person, time and place.

When King Fergus I entered Argyll in AD 503 to set up the Dalriadic kingdom of the Scots, tradition was so strong that he sent for the Stone of Destiny, which was brought from Ireland to the holy island of Iona so that it could be used in his coronation. For the next 400 years, the stone remained in Iona, still being an essential factor in the making of kings. In the tenth century, its travels began again. It was moved from Iona to the abbey of Scone, where Scottish kings were crowned. Edward I, King of England, Hammer of the Scots, in pursuit of his title to Scotland, seized the stone and brought it to Westminster, where it remains in use to this day in confirming the title of the monarch at his or her coronation.

The Stone of Destiny is not, as one might imagine, placed on the omphalos of England, as that site is now forgotten or hidden until the right time comes for it to be revealed. It is beyond dispute that such a centre existed, and was recognized as such. As early as the seventh century of the Christian era, Bede referred to the site as 'Angli Mediterranei', the Middle of the Land of England. In his time the centre was taken to be at Lichfield, on the site of the present cathedral of St Mary and St Chad. The name of Lichfield is said by etymologists to mean 'field of corpses', for here it was supposed a massacre of Christians by pagans occurred at some now forgotten date. The cathedral itself was originally dedicated only to St Chad, a christianization of Mars or one of his Celtic counterparts. March 2nd, the feast day of St Chad, was formerly the day dedicated to the worship of Mars. The spear, Mars's sacred weapon, is admirably suited to pin down the forces on a major omphalos.

In Saxon terms, Mars was equivalent to the god Tiw, patron god of England. Additional evidence for Lichfield Cathedral's central role was seen in the ancient ceremony of beating the bounds which was once performed there. In that ceremony, the eight holy wells around the boundary were visited in turn. Each well represented one of the eight cosmological directions, the four cardinal points and their intermediates. These eight directions are found elsewhere in British tradition as the four Royal Roads of Britain. There have however been other claimants for the title of Omphalos of England such as the Red Horse of Tysoe, a hill figure destroyed in the eighteenth century by the enclosure of the common land upon which it was cut. It was sacred to Tiw, who as the equivalent of Mars gave his name to Tuesday in the English calendar.

The crossroads at Dunstable, where King Edward I set up a memorial cross to his late queen Eleanor, has an even better claim to the status of centre. The town of

Dunstable was set up as a 'plantation' by Edward I. Its preeminent position around the centre was acknowledged by the names of the four main streets, North Street, East Street, South Street and West Street. In geomantic terms, the town was a microcosmic representation of the whole country, the country itself being a microcosmic representation of the world with its quadripartite division. Unlike any other town in England, Dunstable was granted exceptional freedoms and exemption from taxation equal to those enjoyed by the City of London. In addition to these privileges, the right of sanctuary, usually operative only on the consecrated ground of churches and cathedral closes, was granted within the borough. These remarkable exceptions to the rule indicate that Dunstable was held in special regard by King Edward I as the omphalos of his kingdom – the origin point of the Royal Roads.

Oxford, considered by some to be the intellectual capital of England, was also claimed as the actual centre of the country according to the ancient Welsh tale, 'Lludd and Llefelys', in the *Mabinogion*. Three plagues had befallen Britain, the second of which took the form of a scream which was heard each May Eve over every hearth in the land. This horrifying sound terrorized the people, animals and trees, wreaking untold havoc.

King Lludd, wishing to end this disastrous plague, consulted Llefelys who told him that the scream was caused by two dragons who fought over the exact centre of Britain each May Eve. As each hearth was itself the omphalos of each house, the point around which family life was centred, the conditions prevailing at the national omphalos were reproduced there. Lludd therefore had the island measured in length and breadth in order to determine the centre, which was found to be at Oxford. This is an interesting reference to the use of surveying in antiquity in order to find an omphalos. The force had not yet been fixed, but the day and time of its manifestation was known. At the defined point, Lludd had a pit dug. In the pit was set a barrel of the best mead, covered with silk. At the appointed time, the dragons appeared, and fought in the air. After the fight had continued for some time the dragons became weary and sank to the barrel, where they drank the mead and fell asleep. When they were asleep, Lludd wrapped the covering around them and the barrel, which he had transported to Dinas Emrys. Here, the dragons and barrel were buried in a stone coffer.

The Lludd legend is an archetypal tale which demonstrates the connection between the powers of the dragon and an active centre on the earth. Here, the point was made doubly powerful by the intersection of two dragons' powers, and their conflict was harmful to the whole nation. Lludd, the priest king, binds the powers into the earth at the correct point, found by mechanical surveying, and nullifies their energies. The harnessing of the untamed energies is achieved by a special person in a special place by a special method. Such a correspondence of person, place, time and technique is easily recognizable to any practitioner of magic.

When the centre had been defined, the surrounding areas could then be laid out in relation to it. The earlier shrines of the countryside, hills, springs and stones, were incorporated as much as possible into the new order and converted to conform with the new religious system instituted at the conversion of the omphalos.

The centralized complex surrounding the omphalos became the focus of the life of the emergent nation. No longer were the small local shrines deemed to be of great importance. Instead, they became subordinate to the central shrine, incorporated in the national temple which was later to act as a focus for the capital city.

Divination and definition of boundaries

4

From the earliest times, when man began altering the primeval features of the landscape in the pursuit of agriculture, boundaries have been drawn between areas of different usage. A single homestead surrounded by its plot of land might not require any precise definition of its size and area, but adjoining pieces of land belonging to different owners certainly did. The apportionment of newly cleared land to several potential owners, and the checking of boundaries between plots, required a method available to all. The simplest boundaries were natural features: rivers, streams, coastlines, ridges and hills; and to this day many primary boundaries, such as county or national boundaries, are still formed by such features. But these are generally too crude and inflexible for the intricate complexities of human life, and soon completely artificial methods of land division were established, involving the use of measure and number.

If boundaries were to be maintained unchanged against the forces of dissolution, natural, human or supernatural, some sort of definition was essential. They were to be marked in a permanent or semi-permanent way, in relation to independent reference points which could be used, if necessary, to verify and renew the boundary's course. Positions of boundaries were primarily defined by natural features and forces, reinforced by the placing of sticks, stones, trees, ditches, hedges and walls. As they were defined by divinatory methods, including dowsing and astronomical sighting, the lines related directly to the forces in the earth and heavens. Moreover, these same divinatory methods could be used at a later date to check whether the boundary had been correctly maintained and was still performing its geomantic function of marking and dividing the earth. The direct relationship of the boundaries with natural features and the psychic attributes of the place was a concrete expression of the belief, underlying all aspects of geomancy, that any modification of the land must accord with the natural order laid down by the Creator.

The initial construction of boundaries, the enclosure of hitherto open space, was carried out with rituals and sacrifices. It was believed that these sacrifices were necessary to placate or neutralize the guardian spirits of the place, which would otherwise punish man for restricting their liberties. Interference with the original condition of the land was kept at as low a level as possible, in order that its natural attributes might be permitted to function unhindered. The shapes of individual enclosures, if made incorrectly, might wreck a whole scheme, channelling malevolent energies which would hinder the growth of crops, cripple livestock and create disharmony in human affairs. Geomancy aimed to enhance the inherent properties of the favourable place divined by the augur – amplifying rather than modifying. In the case of unfavourable tendencies, the intention was to reduce or nullify the malevolent influence.

Once a boundary was created, a special place was made, set aside in space and time from the surrounding, undefined, areas. The inauguration of such a special area, whether a sacred fane, a homestead or a city, was an act which in microcosmic form paralleled the creation of the world – the setting up of a new order. In the case of towns, planned according to the archetypal image of the cosmic city, the parallel was even more explicit, so it is not surprising to find that the Roman calendar commenced with the foundation day of the city of Rome.

The simplest form of continuous artificial boundary is the ditch, a deepening of the plough furrow. In ancient Greece, and later in Rome, the laying out and

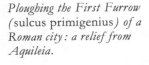

Ploughing the First Furrow (sulcus primigenius) *of a Roman city: a relief from Aquileia.*

defining of the bounds of cities were done by means of ploughing between the four corner markers which had been set up by the geomancer. The plough team was driven around the site, creating the *sulcus primigenius* – the primary furrow. At the plough was a government representative, who held it obliquely so that the earth fell inwards towards the centre of the enclosure. The plough was lifted free of the earth over the areas intended as gateways, so that no interruption of the surface had ever existed on the roads leading through the boundary at these points. The *sulcus primigenius* was then laid out with the appropriate boundary stones, and areas within the city, now officially founded, were allocated by the drawing of lots, involving the hand of fate, rather than the backhand of influence, to decide who should have the best plots of the city.

Viking graves are enclosed by magical shields of stone, mainly in ship or vesica form, at Lindholm, Denmark.

An elaborately carved wagon from Oseberg, Norway, discovered in 1904, may have been used for special ritual journeys of the kind described by Tacitus.

Boundaries were specially contrived with the use of ritual magic to exclude undesirable forces and entities. Consequently the crossing of a sacred boundary without authorization was an act which desecrated the place's sanctity, destroying its psychic shield spiritually if not physically, permitting entry to the unwanted entities. Such an act could only be expiated by death, and those whose entry desecrated Egyptian temples, or who entered the Holy of Holies in the Jewish Temple without permission, were punished by death. Julius Caesar's crossing of the Rubicon, the boundary river of Italy, constituted in Roman law an irreversible act of invasion and was therefore considered in the same way. The preservation of the bounds was irrevocably tied up with the destiny of the people, the fertility of the fields and the fecundity of livestock, so their breach was a psychic attack on those things which were essential for survival. As late as the eighteenth century, the rules of siege stated that a town or city must surrender to the enemy if a 'practicable breach' in the wall – one large enough for the army to march through – was made. Once the bounds had been breached to that extent, all was lost, and further conflict was futile.

Having been laid down, the bounds of an area were kept in the popular consciousness and maintained by ritual walks, 'perambulations', on certain sacred days of the year – perhaps originally related to the day the boundary was established. The best recorded example of such a ritual in ancient times is the Ambarvalia, a Roman festival which survives to this day as the ceremony of 'beating the parish bounds'. At the Ambarvalia, the Magister Pagi, an annually appointed official invested with the powers of the priestly office, led the local inhabitants in a procession along the boundary line, visiting holy groves, stones and altars which marked the way. In the main the altars were dedicated to Silvanus, the deity of the fields, the homestead and the Orientalis – the sacred grove on the boundary. A sheep, a pig and a bull were driven thrice around the fields, after which they were sacrificed. Originally, this threefold sacrifice was made in honour of Mars, but by the time of the emperor Augustus it had become dedicated to Ceres, with the intention of ensuring a successful harvest. In north Europe, the Roman sacrifices to Ceres were paralleled by the sacred circuit of the holy island of Walcheren by the fertility goddess Nehalennia. Of this ritual, Tacitus writes:

In an island in the ocean stands a sacred grove, and in the grove stands a carriage draped with a cloth that none but the priest may touch. The priest can feel the presence of the Goddess in this Holy of Holies, and attends her, as her carriage is drawn by oxen with great ceremony around the island.

Similar fertility-inducing carriage processions were held in honour of Frey by the Norse priesthood.

Terminus, the Roman protector of boundaries, was honoured at the Terminalia, a festival in which his symbol, a phallic post or standing stone marking the boundary, was garlanded by the cultivators of the adjoining land, each on his own side of the post or stone, in acknowledgement of the continuation of the boundary. Such garlanding of phallic objects at the appropriate time of the year was carried out in order to reinvigorate their properties, which had been used up over the previous season.

When pagan worship was banned by an edict of the emperor Theodosius in A D 391, the perambulation of boundaries became incorporated into Christian ritual, as such an efficacious practice could hardly be abandoned without incurring disaster. Thus the Ambarvalia became transformed into the Rogationtide ceremony which redefined the parishes of the new churches – 'beating the parish bounds', a ritual still observed in many places. So strong was its power, intended to preserve the geomantically defined boundaries and hence to promote fertility, that even during the English Reformation, when fanatics wrecked churches, shattered tombstones, demolished stone crosses and desecrated churchyards, the custom was maintained. An injunction of Queen Elizabeth I (1565) on Ancient General Customs reads: '. . . The people shall once a year with their curate walk about the parish as they

were accustomed . . . the curate in certain convenient places shall admonish the people to give God thanks.'

These 'convenient places' were, of course, the ancient markers, the gospel oaks, thorns or yew trees, boundary stones, crosses and their sites, all geomantically sited remnants of a former age.

The boundaries of most parishes must seem to the impartial observer to be irrational or even downright perverse. The unusual courses of many boundary lines are shown by several curious recorded features from bounds which are no longer ceremonially traversed. These demonstrate a deviation from the 'logical' mechanistic technique using straight-line grids, the parish bounds being determined by direct divinatory methods. For example, at Hornshayne, an old house on a *trifinium* (junction of three parishes) in Farway, East Devon, the participants in the ceremony made a small boy crawl along an old beam in the roof, in order that the boundary might be followed in its entirety. This ritual was last enacted on 7 May 1884, a period when many old country traditions intimately connected with the land and its fertility were dwindling because of industrialization and the consequent depopulation of the countryside. At Coly House, Colyford, South Devon, the parish boundary intersected a wall where there was a hole through which a child was required to climb. Both Hornshayne and Coly House obviously dated from a period when the finer points of geomancy were no longer understood (otherwise the houses would not have been built at such sites), yet the traditional ceremonies were still observed as a necessity to ensure the continuity of the guardian boundary.

Before starting the walk, it was customary for each participant in the ceremony of beating the bounds to cut a wand of willow, withy or hazel, for the purpose of striking, and hence re-energizing, the boundary stones and other markers. Children in the party were always beaten with the wands at important landmarks, bumped against stones, or thrown into ditches and ponds where the boundary crossed them. Boys were stood upon their heads on stones and in 'crosses' – shallow cross-shaped trenches dug at traditional sites specifically for the purpose. These trench rituals are probably a memory of human sacrifice performed when the boundary was originally laid out at those places. On each perambulation, a different boy was put in each cross, as it was obviously impossible to sacrifice somebody twice. In Celtic times, human sacrifice sometimes involved ritual drowning or burial in a shaft in the ground. The Gundestrup Bowl, an ancient Celtic

Making a 'cross', a cross-shaped mark trench, during the Riding of the Bounds at Selkirk, Scotland.

Above, *a human sacrifice
depicted on the Iron Age
Gundestrup Bowl, showing the
victim being cast head first into a
shaft or cauldron, is reflected in
the Beating of the Bounds at
Cottenham, Cambs, 9 May
1977. The only departure from
tradition is in the direction of
sexual equality – the modern
'sacrifice' is a girl.*

cauldron depicting a variety of scenes, shows a figure
being thrust into what is probably a sacrificial shaft of
the kind excavated at Holzhausen, Bavaria, and Long
Wittenham, Berkshire. Such shafts contained votive
offerings, and, according to the Middlesex antiquary,
Sir Montagu Sharpe, were used as mark-points in the
Roman survey of Middlesex. Before passing on to the
next mark-point, each member of the party dropped
in a stone, a survival of the votive offering, and the
cross was filled in.

As late as 1895, 'Urbs Camboritum', a columnist in
the *Cambridge Daily News*, could write of the ceremonies
at Houghton in Huntingdonshire:

Houghton parish being bordered on one side by the Ouse,
some of the 'Rogationing' party have to traverse the bounds
in a boat, and one at least of the party, generally a new
member of the Rogation Guild, is treated to a dip in the river.
... Thus from time immemorial the remembrance of the
water boundary – the scientific frontier – has been 'washed
in'. ... In some country places the rustics believe there is
magic in this business, and that the crops show up better for
this periodical farce, fondly fancying that the goddess of
nature rewards the observance of the custom.

Thus, after almost two thousand years of Christianity, the 'goddess of nature' was still believed in and worshipped in the cause of the promotion of fertility.

Of all the various objects used for permanent boundary markers, the most durable have been stone. Injunctions and taboos against moving the stones have existed wherever they have been set up. In the Commination in the Church of England's Book of Common Prayer, there is a passage, 'Cursed be he who moveth his neighbour's land-mark', referring to the mark-stones which, despite the wholesale destruction of many centuries, continuing to this day, can still be found by the wayside.

Each boundary mark-stone was traditionally identified by a name, reflecting the positioning and personal attributes of the stone. Although most of these individual names are now lost, some lists of boundary markers for certain parishes fortunately still survive. At Okehampton, Devon, which was last ritually perambulated in 1950, the following twelve boundary stones are listed: Iron Gate, Sandy Ford, Outer Dinger, Dinger Ridge, Inner Dinger, Cirtory Clitters, New Bridge, Rough Tor Combe, Hartor Corner, Cullever Steps, Alstock Corner and Symond's Ditch. The tradition of named stones is recorded in the Edda. At the entrance to Eljudnir, the Hall of Hel, daughter of Loki, in Niflheim, was a named door-stone, Drop-to-Destruction. In this case, the stone was a boundary marker which warded off good.

Along roads, which often delineate boundaries, milestones set up by Roman surveyors occasionally doubled as boundary markers, and were carved with the names of the parishes. However, between the fourth century AD and 1663 no milestones were set up in Britain. They became increasingly common with the construction of turnpike roads, until they were made compulsory on most roads by an Act of Parliament in 1744, and on all roads in 1766. Such milestones, now moved or with their inscriptions obliterated, can prove misleading to the unwary fieldworker.

The ritual perambulations of parish or city bounds were generally marked by stones, and the practice of marking pathways or tracks by this means is of considerable antiquity. The great megalithic shrine at Avebury in Wiltshire was formerly approached by two serpentine avenues, each defined by a double row of stones. Only one avenue now survives, but enough of it has been erected in the original position to enable us to judge the avenues' pristine condition. Until a century

The London Stone, traditional omphalos of the City of London, is believed to be of at least Roman origin. Formerly in the wall of St Swithin's church, Canon St (destroyed in the war), it now adorns a bank.

Kit's Coty House, Kent: the terminal point of a megalithic processional way. One of the few remaining processional stones was broken up in 1976.

ago, a processional way marked by megaliths linked Aylesford in Kent with the archaic burial chamber at Kit's Coty House. One of the last of these stones was destroyed as recently as 1976. Perhaps the most interesting and controversial discovery of stone markers along a trackway was that made by Dr E. Rudge, formerly principal of West Ham Technical College. In 1949, whilst checking the work of Alfred Watkins, he discovered the remains of a trackway of considerable length, marked at intervals by conglomerate 'puddingstones'. These flinty stones, a kind of natural concrete, are known locally as breedingstones, motherstones and growingstones, because as they weather the pebbles embedded in the matrix fall out, a phenomenon believed in earlier times to generate the pebbles found in fields. This attribute made them sacred to the Earth Mother goddess. Stones were placed in full view upon hilltops and beside fords, with their spacing and frequency determined by the features of the terrain. Rudge believed that the trackway, which connected Thatcham in Berkshire with Grimes Graves in Norfolk, a neolithic flint mine of utmost importance, was a trade route to and from the mines, and beyond to the coast. However, no fewer than eighteen of the markstones are associated with churches, that at Chesham forming part of a stone circle which was incorporated into the church fabric. It is thus quite possible that this trackway was an ancient processional route of undetermined purpose, or perhaps a series of routes.

Ritually perambulated routes, integrating the man-made and the natural with the intention of harmonizing the activities of the human race with the patterns of time, were not restricted to beating the bounds. Little studied, their routes are scarcely known, but we can determine that they took exactly the same path each time they were performed, as each variation of Morris Dance has its own steps and routes between villages, and annual fairs had their own boundaries and streets, laws and customs. This close adherence to the fine detail of traditional ritual ensured the direct continuity of otherwise readily destroyed boundaries, positions esoterically related to both the macrocosmic order of the heavens, and to the microcosmic reenactment of its active phase in the sacred dance or procession. The gyratory dances associated with geomantically sited maypoles represented the annual whirling of the heavens about the fixed earth, the axle-tree founded on the central place which remains steady and endures while all else moves. The patterns traced upon the ground by the dancers, ever approaching the central pole as the ribbons create interlaced forms, are repeated by the gyres of unicursal labyrinths, whose fixed paths lead, between involuted boundaries, from the external world to the internal. Generally made of earth (though appearing on a variety of objects from Cretan coins to wall-tiles) the turf and pavement forms can usually be walked upon. At least 44 are known to have existed in England alone, and hundreds of others are known from all over the globe.

English turf labyrinths, few of which now remain, are believed to date from the Bronze Age or earlier. In design, they have much in common with very ancient rock-scribings. The most ancient dated labyrinth is that which formerly existed in Egypt, from the middle of the nineteenth century before the present era. It was still there at the time of Herodotus, in the fifth century BC, as he left an account of its magnitude. However, it was a building which, although its function may have been religious or initiatory, was not anything like the turf, stone or pavement labyrinths which are so well known. The Egyptian plan was square, with four entrances, one at each cardinal point. In this respect it was a microcosm of the world in the same way as the other mazes. However, it was not unicursal.

The Cretan labyrinth is naturally the best known of all, not least because of the tale of Theseus and the Minotaur. As the simplest archetype, its pattern is reproduced on numerous coins, the same pattern which has been found in the stone mazes of Finland, in the symbolism of the Hopi tribes of North America, and, in more complex forms, as turf and pavement labyrinths.

The design of many labyrinths reproduces, in the main, the cosmic city layout in tangible form, a plan microcosmically related to the archetypal city (Jerusalem or Troy), which was itself a microcosm of the first concept of the world, whose centre was traditionally Jerusalem. The native American Hopi tribe refer to the labyrinth figure as Mother Earth, being the universal plan of the Creator, protecting an especially sacred spot.

The maze at Saffron Walden in Essex has such a form, being circular with four peripheral 'stations'. Most of the gyres traverse only a quadrant, leaving four baulks across the centre, giving the appearance of the Celtic cross, or fourfold division of the world. This microcosmic reference is not fanciful, as the four quarters of the maze were given the names of the towns to which they point – Newmarket, Cambridge, Stortford and Chelmsford. Perhaps the maze was meant to represent the whole district in microcosm.

The Cretan labyrinth, constructed by Daedalus, perhaps an embodiment of the Great Architect of the Universe, may well have represented the journey of the initiate through the tribulations of life, to the centre, and, overcoming death in the form of the Minotaur, being reborn by means of the 'clue' – the thread which enables the soul to travel from the trial plane to another level of existence.

Labyrinths, being primarily religious objects, were, like wells, menhirs and pagan gods, incorporated into the Christian Church, with examples ranging from the simple key-pattern square spiral at Thornton, Leicestershire, to the world-famous *lieue* or league at Chartres Cathedral. Tradition has it that to tread these labyrinth paths (or to crawl them on bended knees) was held, in Christian times, to be spiritually equivalent to a pilgrimage to Jerusalem. The pilgrimage along the labyrinth, which in the case of Chartres is not, despite its name, a *lieue* (the old French league of 2086.66 metres) but more like 150 metres, would have to be made at times when the currents beneath the omphalos were at their height, e.g. on the church's patronal festivals, or solar solstices. Barefoot, so as to absorb the sacred energies (as one removes one's shoes when entering a mosque), the dance to the centre would be a solemn yet joyous occasion, when enlightenment or spiritual experiences might be received by the pilgrim.

English turf labyrinths, probably originating in the Bronze Age, lead the initiate along a ritual perambulation of spiritual significance. Top, the maze at Alkborough, Lincs.; below, the maze at Sneinton, Notts, which was associated with the chapel and holy well of St Anne. The bulges mark four 'stations' around the periphery.

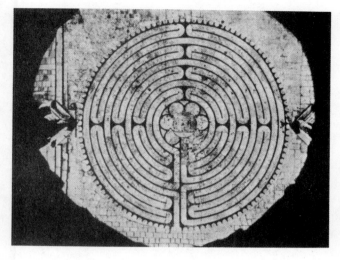

Seen from above, the maze or lieue of Chartres Cathedral, over 40 feet in diameter, once had a Minotaur figure at the centre. Its pattern is identical with that of Alkborough (see opposite, above).

In turf and pavement labyrinths, the patterns of forces in the earth below are translated into material form, two-dimensional renderings of the waterline spirals below and tourbillons, vortices of energy, above. Tourbillons are the transition places from the physical to the astral world, whose points of support are generated by the sacred dance on the sacred omphalos.

On these multiple levels, physical, psychological, spiritual and astral, the labyrinth acts as a boundary between various states of being, preventing the unauthorized from treading on the holy place, defining its nature to the initiate, acting as a practical channel of energy for the adept.

Not defined by drawn figures or earthworks, but equally real, are the processional paths inside sacred edifices. In many Roman Catholic churches there is the ritual of the Stations of the Cross, where the congregation reenact the sacred drama of the last hours of Christ. Again, the imitative element is in evidence, reproducing the events at a certain time, in a certain place, in a certain way. Thus we can detect common features which link together all these religious processions, from the redefinition of boundaries, through the pilgrimage, to the burial of the dead and the reenactment of sacred history.

In order that malevolent influences might be excluded, and that fertility and well-being might be promoted, such consecrated boundaries were set up which had to be maintained intact. However, a boundary with no access points defeats its own object, in that nothing can enter or leave. To overcome this, and yet to maintain the effectiveness of the boundary,

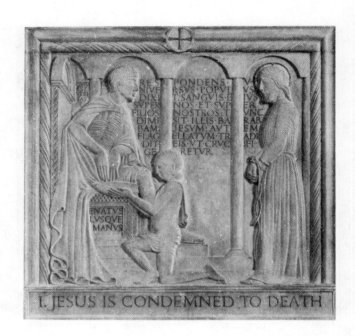

I. JESUS IS CONDEMNED TO DEATH

The first Station of the Cross at Westminster Cathedral: Pilate washes his hands. The carving is by Eric Gill, 1913–18.

special places were set aside as points of entry. These entrances, placed where the plough had been lifted during the ritual of the *sulcus primigenius*, were gaps in the protective enclosure, and hence susceptible to attack. To protect them, they were shielded by guardian devices, flanked by consecrated poles, pillars, obelisks or effigies, and adorned with magical carvings.

Gateways in all cultures were protected by such special devices. Chinese practitioners of Feng-Shui, believing that spirits travelled in straight lines, combated them by making winding paths to prevent demons from approaching temple doors. For additional protection, they constructed a spirit wall in front of the entrance, creating a corner unnegotiable by straight-line fliers. Shinto shrines in Japan were protected by *torii*, gates of entry with a form similar to the Stonehenge trilithons, the Gate of the Sun at Tiahuanaco, Christian lychgates, the entrance to Buddhist stupas and ancient Egyptian pylons. Each Shinto enclosure has three *torii*, the first marking the entrance to the sacred precincts, the second and third being between the first and the Holy of Holies, a hierarchical reinforcement of guardianship. Additional protection was afforded in Japanese and Chinese temple precincts by the presence of running water, channelled into tortuous courses and traversed at special points by humpbacked bridges which traditionally the spirits could not cross.

Of great influence in the Western mystery tradition were the two sacred guardian pillars which flanked the entrance of the Temple in Jerusalem constructed by Solomon. Being on important geomantic points, their ornament, of nets and wreaths of chequerwork, symbolized their tying down of the earth's energies at that point. Named Boaz and Jachin, they represented the immovable pillars which support the sky and the Gates of Dawn, gates to the underworld which exclude the demons and wraiths from entering this world of their own volition. The two holy pillars have been consciously reproduced ever since in many buildings constructed in the masonic tradition. Symbolically, they represent the guardians of the arcane secrets.

Almost invariably, sacrificial foundations were laid in gateways, special attention being essential in such important places. Skeletons of sacrificial victims have often been unearthed at entrances to the sacred enclosures. The Celtic Saint Odhran volunteered to be the first person to be buried on the holy island of Iona, to become its spirit guardian. Lest a less worthy person should predecease him, it is said that he was buried alive – a strange custom for Christians, but an obvious survival of pagan lore.

Japanese torii, *entrance gateways serving the magical function of excluding evil, guard the entrance to the mountain sanctuary of Inari, near Kyoto.*

Akin to this sacrificial practice was the placing of severed human heads in gateway niches in Celtic times. The famous Celto-Ligurian sanctuary gateway found at Roquepertuse, Bouches-du-Rhône, France, contained human skulls and was surmounted by a guardian bird of stone. The skulls' presence in the sanctuary, in addition to terrifying the neophyte and preventing the entry of malevolent spirits, ensured that the place remained the permanent residence of the spirits of the departed, who became its guardians. In the absence of human sacrifice, animal skulls performed a similar function.

A survival of this practice was in evidence in London until the eighteenth century, where the gates of the City sported the severed heads of the executed, ostensibly as a warning to other potential malefactors, but also an unconscious continuation of the geomantic practice of guardianship of entrances. Another remnant of this tradition are the carvings of small human heads in the Romanesque and Gothic periods of church architecture. These guard the apertures in church walls, windows and doors. In the correct form, looking towards the door, there is a male head on the left and a female head on the right, an arrangement found in the positions of the holy guardian pillars, Jachin and Boaz, at the entrance to the Temple of Solomon, and in the position of the bridegroom and the bride at Christian weddings.

In addition to their exclusive function, gateways were often orientated to receive the beneficial rays of the sun on special days. From this practice is derived a curious usage whereby doors were used only for certain rituals, or at certain times. In astrological terms, different times have different auspices, and consequently certain guardian doors may only be effective under certain astrological conditions. Originally, a particular door would only be opened on the day of the dedicatory sunrise, so that the sun's rays could enter the sanctuary and reactivate the temple's energies. As the temple had been orientated on the auspicious day, the reopening would reproduce these beneficial conditions. In East Anglia, houses built before the nineteenth century were orientated north-south, a southward-facing door being considered for some forgotten reason unlucky and never put in a building. In country districts, cottages can still be found whose front door is obviously rarely used, tradition being to use it only for weddings and funerals. Even in the Vatican, there is a certain door which is usually sealed, only being opened by the Pope every 25 years as the symbolic and literal opening of a Holy Year. The northward-facing door in English churches was traditionally opened only during baptisms; when the Devil, who was inhabiting the unbaptized infant, left the body, he was supposed to flee through this door to the northern regions which were traditionally his abode. Once expelled through this door, there was no re-entry, as it was closed until the next baptism.

Thus what may appear to be a simple delineation of a special area for worship or habitation in reality incorporated numerous magical processes at each stage of its construction and dedication, with the intent of ensuring safety from psychic attack. The purpose of geomancy was to define and construct such areas in the best method suitable for the place.

Gateways at Tiahuanaco, Bolivia (left), and Isfahan, Iran, are both characterized by magical carvings intended to protect the sacred precinct from malevolent influences.

Images in the earth

5

The ithyphallic Giant of Cerne Abbas, Dorset, over 180 feet in length, is perhaps the only ancient hill figure in the country to have survived virtually unaltered.

Hill figures represent some of the best-known and best-loved landmarks in the country. They are believed to have their origin in the Iron Age, and were usually made by removing a layer of turf to reveal the contrasting white of the chalk underneath. They were therefore restricted in the main to chalk areas: the Downs, Wiltshire, the Chilterns, and the Gog-Magog Hills of Cambridgeshire. In form they are roughly divided into three categories – horses, giants, and abstract figures. Many of the horse figures are of eighteenth-century origin (at least in their present form) but the Bratton (Westbury) and Uffington White Horses are definitely more ancient.

Although the majority are now destroyed or altered out of all recognition from their pristine state, the few hill figures which still survive each represent an impressive feat of design and coordinated execution. Their visibility from great distances has led several writers to suggest that they were primarily intended to be viewed from above, as markers for, or messages to, the gods. In his 1945 book, *The Riddle of Prehistoric Britain*, Comyns Beaumont drew attention to the numerous folk tales concerning human flight in antiquity, and put forward the fantastic theory that the English hill figures may have been markers for prehistoric aviators. This theme was later taken up by UFO enthusiasts, who applied Beaumont's ideas to extraterrestrial visitors.

The theory that some at least commemorated victory in battle is certainly true in the case of the hammer carved on the hillside at Tours in France. This was done on the orders of Charles Martel to celebrate his victory over the Arabs, AD 732. Indeed, as late as 1716 Prince Eugène ordered the fashioning of a hill figure in the form of an eagle to celebrate his capture of the city of Belgrade. This eighteenth-century trophy, at a time when geomancy had been reduced in Europe to minimal survivals, is a continental parallel of the numerous 'aesthetic' white horses and military regimental badges, of which the last to be cut in England was in 1951.

Ancient hill figures, of which the phallic Cerne Abbas giant probably represents the sole unaltered survival, were probably connected with pagan fertility-generating rituals. Of the others still known, Gog-Magog at Cambridge was completely obliterated; the Long Man of Wilmington was recut on the orders of the Duke of Devonshire in 1873; and there is evidence that the Uffington White Horse was formerly more naturalistic. At certain times the figures' surfaces were scoured to prevent vegetation recolonizing the barren surfaces which made the figures visible. At those scourings, festivals with very obvious pagan ceremonies were held, until the nineteenth century destroyed the old ways which necessitated them.

Just as hill figures were constructed in Britain and Europe by removing the turf to reveal the contrasting underlying rock stratum, so the native American tribes made their figures in the form of low earthwork mounds. Our knowledge of them is solely archaeological, as the inhabitants of the regions where they are found were exterminated before their purpose could be transmitted to the new inhabitants of America. Before they were largely destroyed for agricultural reasons, many of the North American 'effigy mounds' as they have come to be called, were surveyed between the 1820s and the 1840s by S. and R. C. Taylor, J. Locke, E. H. Davis and E. G. Squier, who recorded them with many fine engraved plans.

A wide range of effigies once existed, ranging in form from an orientated cross with 25-foot-long arms at Tarlton, Ohio, to octagonal ritual enclosures with sides of 800 feet at Portsmouth in the same state. At Adams County, Ohio, there is the famous, and thankfully still preserved, Great Serpent Mound. Along the 'Great Indian Trail' or 'War Path' from the Mississippi to Lake Michigan were various groups of animal and human effigies, several being laid out on obvious alignments. The common feature of these effigies is that most of them can only be interpreted from above – that is, from the air.

Precisely this method was required before the now famous figures and lines of Nazca in Peru were revealed to the world. Until this parched terrain was photographed from the air, the inhabitants of the area had for centuries ignored the network of criss-crossing furrows and grooves which made no coherent sense, even if anybody had bothered to attempt their interpretation.

Overleaf, *North American effigy mounds, once widespread but now almost all demolished by treasure hunters and others:* left, *the 2000-year-old Great Serpent Mound of Ohio as it appears today, and (*right*) as it was sketched by Squier and Davis in 1846. Below, a group of effigy mounds in Wisconsin, as surveyed by Taylor and Locke (1848).*

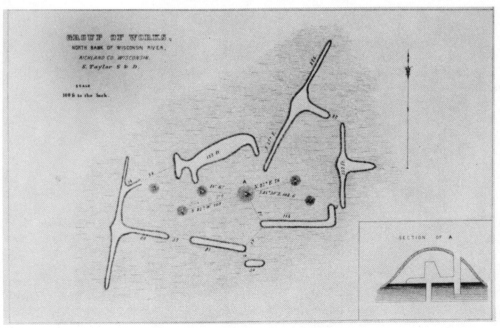

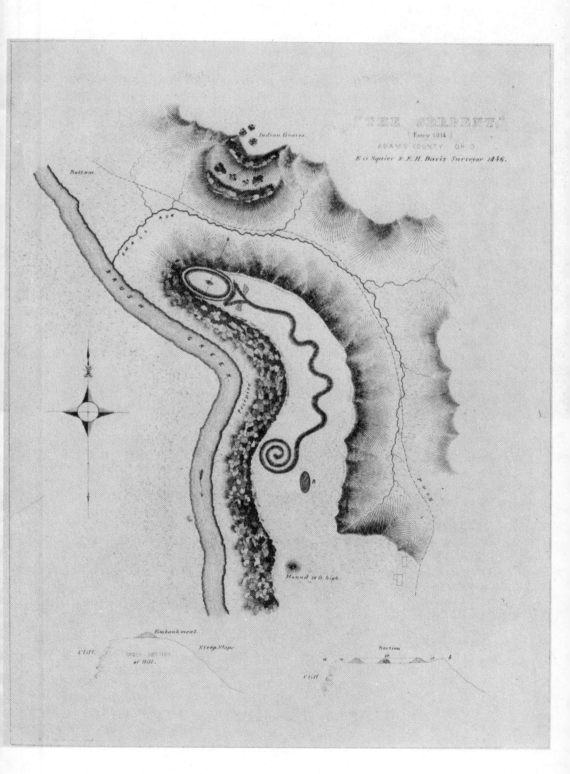

"THE SERPENT"
[Entry 1014]
ADAMS COUNTY OHIO
E G Squier & E H Davis Surveyor 1846.

Indian Graves.

Bottom.

SMALL RUN

BRUSH CREEK

Prairie.

B

Mound 20 ft. high.

Embankment.

Cliff.   CROSS SECTION   Steep Slope.
of Hill.

Section

Cliff.

73

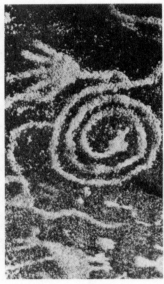

The *Nazca spider, a large figure scratched on the Peruvian* pampa *and visible only from the air, was drawn with such accuracy that the species (not a local variety) can be immediately identified by experts.* Above, *a spiral from a South American painting microcosmically repeats the much larger spirals on the ground at Nazca.*

The aerial camera brought them immediately into perspective, showing them to be in reality an interconnected system of lines making up complex and beautifully planned figures of humans, birds, fishes, lizards and monkeys. The design of a spider is so clearly depicted that arachnologists have been able to determine the species, one found only in the Amazon forests beyond the Andes. Recent work has suggested that the figures represent the Nazca peoples' interpretation of celestial constellations.

Perhaps the most interesting observation to emerge from the discovery of the Nazca lines and figures is that both lines and figures seem to be merged in a coherent, although still only partially understood, system. This appears to parallel closely the system which may be inferred in Europe in the light of discoveries made by various geomantic researchers like Black, Watkins, Maltwood, Heinsch and Edwards.

At several places in England and Wales, the configurations of road and track, river and ditch, field boundaries and woods, have seemed to represent the form of vast figures. Sometimes several miles in length, these figures are variant forms of the familiar signs of the zodiac. Here a bull, there a remarkably lifelike fish or scorpion, are placed with a precision and completeness which belie any suggestions of randomness, but which demonstrate the practice of a highly developed form of geomantic construction. A synthesis of divination, survey and landscape engineering subtly links the natural forms of the earth's surface with the artificial forms of the human consciousness to create a total geomantic landscape – the aim of geomancers throughout the world.

The first of these zodiacs to be identified was at and around Glastonbury. The sculptress Katherine Emma Maltwood (1878–1961) discovered it completely by accident during her research into the legends and traditional sites associated with King Arthur. In tracing out the routes and places of the Grail quest on Ordnance Survey maps, Maltwood noticed that the River Cary between Somerton and Charlton Mackerell seemed to form the shape of the underside of a lion. Continuing the figure, she traced out a complete animal. Further work on maps and subsequent work in the field convinced her that she had rediscovered King Arthur's Round Table. According to the Norman book *La Queste de Sangraal* the Round Table was laid out by Merlin, whose legendary geomantic works at Stonehenge have been recounted by Geoffrey of Monmouth.

In the *High History of the Holy Grail* it was said that the Round Table could feed 4,000 people and 150 bulls, being none other than the famous twelve hides of Glaston given to Joseph of Arimathea by King Arviragus.

Maltwood thus believed the Glastonbury zodiac to be the enshrinement in the earth of an archetypal set of myths, originally pre-Christian, from which the tales associated with King Arthur and the Knights of the Round Table were derived. As long as the zodiac at Glastonbury was the only known example, the connection seemed feasible. Now, after the discovery of several more terrestrial zodiacs, the theory seems less tenable. Perhaps the legends were a religious enactment of sacred history which took place at the appropriate point and time in each zodiac.

In *Terrestrial Zodiacs in Britain*, the discoverer of the Pendle zodiac, Professor Robert Lord, has written:

The precise purpose of the British terrestrial zodiacs we may never be able to rediscover. But with the further accumulation of knowledge, it should be possible within a few years from now to build up a general theory of their significance. This will be particularly so if prejudices against their acceptance can be overcome. It will be especially significant if zodiacs are found in parts of Europe where detailed recorded histories go back further than in Britain. One thing we can be certain of is that the construction of these zodiacs was no passing whim of a semi-primitive people. To project sophisticated drawings onto a landscape, to arrange them in a particular order, and to incorporate natural features such as rivers and streams, would require very considerable surveying skill, a degree of skill that would make much modern surveying seem mere child's play. Some then must have taken several generations to complete; and the dedication and ingenuity put into them cannot have been surpassed even by the cathedral builders of medieval times. If the reader wishes to gain some inkling of the magnitude of the task, he could make a beginning by trying to project a drawing of a human or animal figure on to his back garden or lawn from his back door. He will discover that it is by no means easy, whether he uses stones or bricks, or even a lawn-mower.

In 1948, Lewis Edwards found another zodiac. At Pumpsaint in South Wales was the 'Welsh Temple of the Zodiac', now commonly referred to as the Pumpsaint zodiac. Only a brief outline of his findings are published, in the form of three short articles in the magazine *Research* and its successor *Atlantean Research*. The general layout of the zodiac conforms with that at Glastonbury, the only major variation being that Aquarius is represented by a squirrel instead of an eagle or phoenix. His definitive work on the zodiac was

Left, *the planispheric circle of the Glastonbury zodiac, ten miles in diameter, as interpreted by Mary Caine. The rectangle encloses the area shown in the aerial photograph (opposite), showing the effigy of Gemini at Dundon surrounded by the ship* Argo Navis. *Woods and earthworks form the head, and ancient lynchets delineate the figure's ribs. The whole effigy of Gemini is about two miles in length.* Below, *the Leo effigy from the Nuthampstead zodiac in Hertfordshire. All Leo effigies so far discovered resemble those found at Glastonbury and Nuthampstead.*

complete but unpublished at the time of his death in 1956, and his manuscripts are believed to be lost.

Since 1960, a number of zodiacs have been discovered, including one at Kingston-on-Thames which Mary Caine has written about; Nuthampstead, Hertfordshire, found by the author in 1969; Ongar, Essex, discovered by Jim Kimmis; Stanley, Durham; Holderness, Yorkshire, and Bury St Edmunds, Suffolk. Several others have been stated to exist, although evidence is fragmentary or merely heresay. Amongst these are Wirrall (unlikely owing to changes in coastline), Banbury, Hampshire and Edinburgh. Donald Cyr, an American researcher into astro-archaeology, found a Virgo effigy in Eire on the parallel 52° North, on which the Nuthampstead, Banbury, Pumpsaint and Preseli zodiacs are to be found. A zodiac has also been found at Verdon in France, where Tibetan lamas have set up a monastery. The zodiacs' positions appear to be precisely sited, in the manner of Stonehenge or Arbor Low, and represent the result of painstaking survey. Emerging evidence suggests that the country in former times may have been divided into geomantic provinces or dioceses, each of which contained a zodiac, just as later the Christian Church divided the country into dioceses under the authority of bishops. Interestingly, the known zodiacs fit the present ecclesiastical dioceses to a remarkable degree, so it is possible to speculate that they may have functioned as the equivalent of cathedrals, each part being used at the appropriate time of the year.

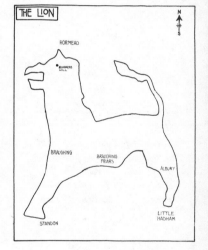

THE LION

HORMEAD

BUMMERS MILL

BRAUGHING

BRAUGHING FRIARS

ALBURY

STANDON

LITTLE HADHAM

6

Geomancy and the geometry of the land

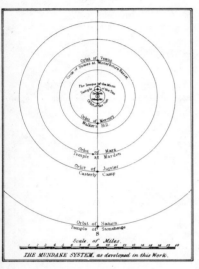

The first published alignment of ancient sacred sites. Although inaccurate, the Rev. Duke's system was a forerunner of the work of Black, Bennett, and Alfred Watkins.

The harmonious balance of the elements which compose the landscape has long been recognized by poets and painters as a seemingly intangible essence which controls and forms the visible outward relationships. A mysterious pattern is concealed within the countryside, recognizable, yet indefinable.

Almost everybody will agree that certain places on the earth's surface seem more agreeable or inspiring than others, and these places have often become centres of worship. The sites of megalithic and later shrines have also appeared to be centres of exceptional power, but the question of inter-relationship has remained obscure. A corpus of evidence which indicates that many centres of power are geometrically related to one another has been painstakingly pieced together by numerous professional and amateur researchers over the last century or so.

As early as 1845 the Rev. E. Duke, in his book *The Druidical Temples of the County of Wilts*, wrote of the meridional (i.e. north-south) alignment which he supposed to run for sixteen miles from the stone circle at Winterbourne Bassett through Avebury, Silbury Hill, Walker's Hill, and Easterly Camp to Stonehenge. He believed each site to have been a temple dedicated to a different astrological 'planet', i.e. to Venus, the Earth, the Sun, Mercury, Mars, Jupiter and Saturn – an astrological parallel with the Seven Wonders of the World. As far as can be ascertained, Duke was the first researcher to publish an attempted alignment of ancient sites. His interpretation remains enigmatic, though it showed a grasp of one of the essential points in geomancy – the relation of objects on the surface of the earth to the astronomical phenomena above, as in the Hermetic maxim 'As above, so below'.

William Henry Black had also been working since the 1820s on ancient alignments, though he divulged little publicly until a couple of years before his death in 1872. Historiographer at the Public Record Office in London, Black discovered systems of aligned sites all over Britain. Owing to the belief then prevalent that the Britons and Saxons were savages, he attributed these alignments to the activities of Roman survey engineers. On Tuesday 6 September 1870, at the Green Dragon Hotel, Hereford, he read his most important paper to a meeting of the British Archaeological Association. In it he expounded his discoveries of the terrestrial geometry of Herefordshire, explaining that Credenhill, which he claimed had been a camp of Roman engineers, defined by distant mark-points, was the centre of what would now be called the geomancy of the county of Hereford. From this point, geometrical lines linked up with other important earthworks and landmarks throughout Britain:

Monuments exist marking grand geometrical lines, [he wrote] lines which cover the whole of Western Europe, extending beyond Britain to Ireland, the Hebrides, the Shetlands, the Orkneys, right up to the Arctic Circle. These lines are all carried out on a principle which I have had the happiness of detecting. . . . But this system is more ancient than the Roman Empire, and goes far wider. It exists in India, China, and the provinces of the east, which are all laid out in the same way.

However much or little the work of Black may have influenced later researchers into terrestrial geometry, it is interesting on two counts, namely that it was given under the aegis of the British Archaeological Association, and that the paper was read in the home town of a later and much better-known researcher into alignments – Alfred Watkins. As Black's findings were publicized only shortly before his death, nothing was ever published in book form. Apart from records of his lectures in various journals and society proceedings, all else, including his maps of the alignments, is now lost.

A later researcher, F. J. Bennett, noted that the remains of megalithic structures at Coldrum and Addington, Kent, were on a north-south alignment, as were Kit's Coty House and the Countless Stones. Traditionally, the Coldrum to Addington alignment was reputed to have been an ancient religious processional way, marked along its length by megaliths, though most have now been destroyed by farmers. On checking various sites in Kent to ascertain whether these 'meridional lines' were general, Bennett found many of them, and published ten such lines. In the Wealden Forest, he noted that the lines tended to be east-west rather than north-south.

His researches on Kentish megaliths led to the discovery that many of them, being of pagan sanctity, were used in the foundations of churches. Others remained in situ in the churchyards, or occurred in the countryside at regular intervals of a mile. His method was a forerunner of that adopted seventeen years later by Alfred Watkins, using the same mark-points: camps, tumuli and churches. The degree of accuracy stipulated by Watkins was greater than Bennett's, however, as Bennett believed that the church positions were sometimes 'pulled off' the alignment by topographical features such as rivers and valleys.

Workers in this field at or about this time include Hadrian Allcroft, the Scottish antiquary Ludovic McLellan Mann, and Sir Norman Lockyer, the great astronomer-scientist and virtual founder of astro-archaeology. All these researchers found a common and recurrent theme: apparently deliberate geometrical figures and alignments laid out across the countryside.

Alfred Watkins, whose work is better known today than at any time since its publication, coined a new word to describe these alignments of ancient sites. He called them leys, giving sound reasons for his choice, and set up a society to further their study, the Old Straight Track Club. Born in 1855, Watkins lived his whole life in Herefordshire, where he became senior partner in a flour-milling company and a pioneer in photographic technology. (The 'Watkins Factor' was used for years as a standard method of calculating processing times in developing photographs, and he also invented and patented a light meter.)

Watkins's rediscovery of ancient aligned sites was first publicized through the Woolhope Naturalists' Club, one of the many associations of antiquaries and naturalists which were so popular in the late nineteenth and early twentieth centuries. Members of the Woolhope Naturalists' Club travelled to interesting places for picnics and lectures, as well as carrying out the work of documenting many ancient sites and making excavations. Watkins's photographs can be found through all the Woolhope publications of the period, and are of exceptional quality. Some are even in colour.

Watkins's rediscovery of ancient alignments occurred on 30 June 1921. 'A visit to Blackwardine,' he later wrote, 'led me to note on the map a straight line starting from Croft Ambury ... over hill points, through Blackwardine, over Risbury Camp, and through the high ground of Stretton Grandison, where I surmise a Roman station. I followed up the clue of sighting from hilltop ... the straight lines to my amazement passing over and over again through the same class of objects.'

Alfred Watkins's own photograph (c. 1920) of a Bristol ley from Broad St, which runs down the street and through an archway under St John's church, continuing to St Michael's church on the hill beyond.

Watkins believed that his leys were ancient trackways, laid out by surveyors by means of ranging lines with sighting poles. The intention, he believed, was to mark out ways for itinerant merchants, certain tracks being for the transport of specific commodities such as salt or flints. But this did not explain why ley lines occasionally traversed impossible terrain, sometimes going up the sides of mountains and across bogs. The point was taken up by later researchers, who claimed that the lines must have had an alternative purpose.

All this was the start of a considerable amount of research by Watkins, who developed his thesis in a number of books, bringing forth much evidence, mainly from fieldwork, to back up his conclusions. Unfortunately, the established archaeologists found Watkins's work totally unacceptable, an attitude which, despite increasing evidence from numerous diverse sources, they have never felt necessary to change.

As already mentioned, to explore the subject, Watkins founded the Old Straight Track Club, which by means of postally circulated portfolios (now preserved in Hereford Museum) disseminated members' views and discoveries. After Watkins's death in 1935, the club continued until the late 1940s, when it petered out. In 1939, Major F. C. Tyler, a member of the club, published *The Geometrical Arrangement of Ancient Sites*, where he demonstrated the circles he had discovered in various places, along with a metrological analysis of terrestrial geometry.

A small amount of research continued after the war. In 1948, K. H. Koop found that an equilateral triangle system incorporating Stonehenge, noted by Sir Norman Lockyer, could be extended across the whole of Salisbury Plain. But interest in terrestrial geometry began to wane from the 1940s, to the delight of conventional archaeologists, who had been against the line of research since its inception. The theories and works of Alfred Watkins and his followers had apparently been consigned to the waste bin, never to reappear. There was no way, it seemed, that geomantic research could ever be restarted in such a climate of positive materialism in the wake of the nascent nuclear age. 'Occultism', with which terrestrial geometry had become associated in the popular mind, had been all but discredited by science and, to make matters worse, the defeated Nazis had been found to have subscribed to certain branches of occultism, including geomancy, producing 'guilt by association'.

But from the USA came strange reports. Lights in the sky, formerly dismissed as hallucinations or worse, were being reported with increasing frequency. Fears that they might be enemy secret weapons led to a spate of official government investigations, and a new popular name was coined – flying saucers.

Now this is not the place to discuss the observations, discoveries and hypotheses surrounding the phenomena. Many books and magazines have appeared explaining, or purporting to explain flying saucers, or, as the United States Air Force soon named them, Unidentified Flying Objects. This name was soon shortened to the acronym UFO, which is now in universal use. Whatever their origins, many observers in Europe and America observed that these so-called UFOS appeared to travel in straight lines, and, in the late 1950s and early 1960s the books of Aimé Michel, especially *Flying Saucers and the Straight-Line Mystery*, again focused attention on the possibility of fixed alignments of paths of energy on the surface of the earth. These lines or 'orthotenies', were soon linked with the earlier discoveries of Watkins, whose major work, *The Old Straight Track*, was still available.

In 1961, Tony Wedd published the booklet *Skyways and Landmarks*, the first publication to link UFO orthotenies with classical Watkins-type alignments, and this connection helped to reawaken interest in Watkins's discoveries. In May 1961, Philip Heselton, inspired by Tony Wedd, set up the Ley Hunters' Club and its organ, the magazine *The Ley Hunter* (later refounded by Paul Screeton, and now published under the editorship of Paul Devereux). These ventures generated even more interest and brought the name Watkins to those who had never heard of or thought about such matters.

The UFO hypothesis also led to the restatement of a theory first postulated in 1938 by Arthur Lawton, which claimed that such alignments carried some sort of force or power. This idea, which is in keeping with much folklore-derived evidence, has been extended by the work of numerous dowsers who have tried their art on alignments found by mapwork. This concept was explored and expanded by John Michell in his books, *The Flying Saucer Vision* (1967), *The View Over Atlantis* (1969), and *The Earth Spirit* (1975). In 1974, his work on the alignments in the Land's End district of Cornwall was published in *The Old Stones of Land's End*, which reappraised the work of Sir Norman Lockyer in the light of Watkins's discoveries. Michell studied the alignments revealed by Lockyer, and found that they could be extended to form classical ley lines. He took into account only standing stones and circles, in order to avoid the criticism often put forward by archaeologists that sites on leys are not of contemporary origin, and thus invalidate the line. Despite this impressive verification of the alignments and their subsequent authentication by means of computers, the archaeological world remained silent.

Also derived from the renaissance of interest in Watkins is the work of John G. Williams, who has named his system of alignments the SCEMB system. This acronym is made up of the initials of classes of objects he counts as legitimate in determining alignments: standing stones, cairns and tumuli, earthworks of pre-Roman date, moats and mounds of pre-Roman date, and burial barrows. The system differs from classical leys by excluding everything of Roman and post-Roman date.

At present, numerous researchers at all levels are attempting to unravel this most complex problem of ancient landscape geometry, its date, origin and purpose. Since 1974 developments have followed from the rediscovery of a whole corpus of material left by researchers in Germany between the two world wars. As in Britain, the pioneering work dates from over a century ago, but the work of the period in question originated with the ideas of Albrecht, a surveying

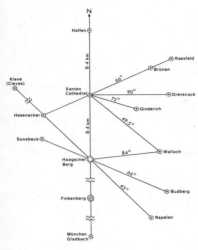

The alignments system incorporating the Haagscher Berg and Xanten Cathedral, W. Germany, as discovered by Josef Heinsch.

engineer killed in the First World War, who made a study of the Stonehenge orientations discovered by Sir Norman Lockyer. Albrecht's ideas were taken up and developed by Father Johann Leugering, who founded the German school of landscape geometers which included Josef Heinsch, Wilhelm Teudt and Kurt Gerlach.

Josef Heinsch, whose achievements in geomantic research put him on a level with Alfred Watkins himself, was also interested in alignments all over Europe and beyond. Heinsch analysed the patterns made by the positions of churches on former pagan sites, and found that they formed part of a network of alignments, each site being at a particular angle to a 'holy hill' or a 'solar site', important religious centres both in pagan and in Christian times. He verified his hypothesis at numerous sites, notably at the Haagscher Berg and the Stoppelberg in Germany, and the complex of stone circles at Odry in Czechoslovakia. Recent work by the Cambridge mathematician Michael Behrend has demonstrated that a comparable system of alignments exists south of Cambridge around the important centre of Wandlebury.

Like most great innovators, Heinsch was criticized by those who could not appreciate his vision. In *Vorzeitliche Ortung in Kultgeometrischer Sinndeutung* (1937), he wrote (Behrend's translation):

The road to this fundamental discovery was not one of those already marked out by our scientific prehistorians, so that they greeted the results with scepticism. It started out – with the definite intention from the first of reaching a proper understanding of the holy hill – from a comparison of Xanten Cathedral with Stonehenge, and in 1933 the author was first able to draw attention to the great north-south axis on the lower Rhine, running from the church hill at Haffeln and over the site of Xanten Cathedral, the Haagscher Berg, the chapel on the Finkenberg, etc., with the 45° line from Cleves to Repelen and the Galgenberg at Meerbeck crossing over the Haagscher Berg, which could be identified as the chief holy hill. The associated solar site (the biblical 'Garden of Eden') lies to the east with the usual deviation of 6°, and is marked as a Christian centre by the church at Wallach, which at the same time is situated at 49.5° (angle of 6:7 right triangle and the axis of the famous sun-temple Stonehenge) to the choir of St Victor's cathedral in Xanten.

Heinsch developed the connection between ancient prehistoric landscape geometry and medieval ecclesiastical building, the inner architectural geometry being seen as a microcosm of the geomancy of the surrounding country. As can be seen from the diagram of the geometry around Xanten Cathedral and the Haagscher

Berg, the discoveries of Heinsch bear a close relationship to the works of Watkins and his predecessors, though they are approached from a different direction incorporating distances and azimuths, a more quantifiable method.

In the same period as Heinsch was Kurt Gerlach, who published geomantic articles in the National Socialist journal *Germanien* between 1940 and 1943, when the magazine ceased publication. As the journal was sponsored by none other than Heinrich Himmler, head of the SS, most of Gerlach's work perished in the flames at the end of the war, and in the post-war destruction of Nazi books. However, not everything was destroyed, and the Institute of Geomantic Research was able to obtain copies of the articles and to save Gerlach's discoveries from oblivion. His work represents an important and early contribution to the reconstruction of the ancient geomantic survey, which appears to have been carried out in Europe from prehistoric times until the late Middle Ages. Gerlach concentrated mainly upon the foundation of Christian shrines in tenth-century Bohemia. He found that Bohemian Benedictine abbeys were constructed on alignments at distances in multiples of 11 km., 44 km. being the old German measure discovered by Father Leugering, the *raste*. A system of landscape geometry based on the citadel at Prague was investigated by Gerlach, who discovered geometrical figures based upon the modular distance of 11 km. Owing to the difficult circumstances under which the research was carried out, it was published in little more than note form, and has never been followed up.

Using Heinsch's discoveries as a basis, the Cambridge mathematician Michael Behrend found, as did many others before him, vast networks of alignments across the British countryside. On statistically analysing his findings he discovered that the places on the alignments were laid out according to multiples of fixed distances, designated by him the x and y units. These are equivalent to 295.3 metres and 464.1 metres respectively. The alignments appear to fit into a system of vast geometrical figures which incorporate the measures with cunning accuracy. Behrend has worked on the famous alignment which links St Michael's on Glastonbury Tor; Gare Hill; the southern corner of Maiden Bradley Priory; the centre of a small landscape geometry figure in the shape of a vesica piscis (a figure formed by the intersection of two circles through each other's centres); the centre of Stonehenge; the eastern

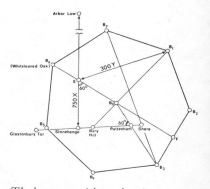

The heptagon with overlapping decagon, the major figure in the landscape geometry of southern Britain. As in the work of Heinsch, significant distances and angles determine the positions of important sites like Stonehenge, and incorporate natural features like Glastonbury Tor.

edge of Bury hill fort; the east edge of Puttenham Common hill fort; Shere church; and a large tumulus in Deerleap wood, west of Dorking in Surrey.

The cultural background

After many years of vehement argument between the proponents and opponents of the claims of men such as Black, Bennett, Watkins and Heinsch, recent work in the young field of astro-archaeology indicates the possible function of such alignments in astronomical observation. But aligned sites and their concomitant connecting straight roads have since early times been fixed in the consciousness of the human race. Biblical references appear to allude to straight pathways laid out in a sacred manner. The tradition also appears to exist in native American lore as the 'red and blue roads'.

Whatever the origin and purpose of such mythological lines, their universality attests to a compelling power over the human mind. But in spite of this irresistible attraction, the sceptic might ask, 'Yes, but where is the documentary evidence?' It is all very well to quote the opinions of antiquaries who may have been equally sincere and misguided, yet were they merely ensnared in a 'mare's nest', as Alfred Watkins quaintly called such a problem?

Until 1939 visible evidence of such alignments crossing large tracts of territory had still not been found, and they therefore could be dismissed as fantasies. In that year, however, Dr Paul Kosok of Long Island University discovered in Peru a vast series of ground drawings. Some were of animal effigies comparable in size and style with those which had been recorded a century earlier by European settlers in North America. The ground drawings, which had been produced in Nazca desert by removing the dark-coloured drifted material from the lighter-coloured subsoil, were connected by a complex and seemingly random pattern of straight lines, at first believed to be the remains of irrigation systems, but soon recognized as a deliberate construction for unknown purposes. The patterns, which have been thoroughly documented by Maria Reiche, who has devoted her life to the task, form a remarkable parallel with the patterns described by Black, Watkins and their successors, as many of them run straight as a die up one side of plateaux and down the other side, just as do the alignments found in Britain. After the Nazca discoveries, other lines were found in Peru and Bolivia, perhaps fragments of a universal system represented by the spirit paths of China and the Royal Roads of England.

The tale of Lludd and Llefelys (see p. 51) suggests that surveying was known in early Britain and was even used to determine the centre of the country. Lines, too, are recorded, as in *The History of the Kings of Britain* by Geoffrey of Monmouth, where King Belinus is said to have called together all the workmen of Britain and commanded that a highway should be built of stone and mortar to cut across the whole length of the island, leading in a straight line from city to city. Across this, a second road was built, and two others in a diagonal pattern, creating the four Royal Roads of England, an eightfold division of the island. Whether Geoffrey's book was based on orally transmitted history, or was merely assembled as a tale incorporating ideas received from folklore, it does at least show that in his time there was a tradition of the construction of the roads to a single plan in ancient times. Geoffrey of Monmouth stated that in addition to constructing the roads, Belinus ratified the laws of his father Dunvallo Molmutius. These so-called Molmutine Laws sanctified the roads of Britain, making all acts of violence committed upon them not merely civil offences but sacrilege. The roads, laid out according to a cosmologically determined plan, were thus sanctified, made inviolable from alteration as carriers of the sacred energies emanating from the centre.

But it must be noted that these lines may be totally different in character from those of Nazca, or those linking the ancient megalithic sites of Europe. They date from a much later period. Like Roman centuriation, they may represent the remodelling of the landscape from its former state of harmony with the natural features to a new image, modelled on the city around the omphalos, microcosm of the world.

A century after Geoffrey of Monmouth put pen to paper, such lines were still in use. By 1220 the Christian religion was well established and, though the earlier pagan rites were doubtless practised by the rural population, the Church was spiritually the dominant power. Edicts suppressing paganism had been issued by many kings, from the time of Edgar and Canute, though witch trials were still a thing of the future. Thus the old knowledge was not yet lost, but the displacement of country beliefs by town-based ideas was well advanced.

At Old Sarum, an Iron Age earthwork, there existed a cathedral city with a considerable population living

Salisbury Cathedral, whose site was said to have been determined by the flight of an arrow in 1220, lies on a major meridional alignment which includes Stonehenge.

cheek by jowl with a military garrison. Relations were far from amicable, and it was decided that the cathedral and its surrounding population would have to be moved elsewhere. Local legend recounts that the site of the new cathedral was determined by the shooting of an arrow from the ramparts of the old city. At the place where the arrow fell to earth, the cathedral was constructed. As this sort of tale is repeated in many places, there may appear nothing remarkable about it. After all, Robin Hood, Little John, Piers Shonkes, Jack O'Legs and many other legendary figures are said to have divined their burial places by such a method. In the case of Salisbury Cathedral, however, there is an important difference. Bennett, in 1904, noted that the cathedral is on an alignment which runs from Stonehenge through Old Sarum and Salisbury Cathedral to Clearbury Ring. It is obvious that the indefinite method of shooting an arrow could not account for the accurate siting of the building on this line, so another solution had to be found.

Medieval navigators and surveyors often used the Jacob's Staff, or baculum, an instrument which was derived from the *dioptra*, a crossbow-like construction with a foresight and a backsight which could be used for accurately sighting along a line and determining angle and distance. Uninitiated observers, viewing a geomancer sighting along the alignment with such an instrument, might well assume that he was holding a crossbow and shooting an arrow from it.

Accurate surveying was well within the capability of the technology of 1220, and in the British Museum there is a complex astrolabe of English manufacture, dated 1187. Scale drawing and mapping were essential to the construction of a vast cathedral like Salisbury, and surviving folklore and topographical evidence indicate that such methods were also applied to the determination of the sites of sacred buildings.

Although this knowledge was a living tradition in 1220, and survived to be practised in the laying out of King's College Chapel in Cambridge by King Henry VI as late as 1446 (see p. 136), the Wars of the Roses and the Reformation largely destroyed and, in the eyes of the new leaders, rendered obsolete such apparently occult techniques. Apart from their survival in a garbled form in folk tradition, and in the physical existence of aligned sites, the corpus of knowledge was expunged from everyday practical use, and new construction went on with little regard for former usages.

The mathematical view

In the light of all the discoveries made during the last century, it has often been claimed that thousands of alignments exist, running across the country in vast profusion but apparently without discernible purpose. The protagonists of this view are usually those who enjoy drawing lines across maps, and, indeed, they are correct, as thousands of lines can be drawn. But several mathematicians have raised the objection that, according to their mathematical models, the number of points available in the given areas may be so plentiful that they will produce alignments which correspond well statistically with those one might expect to be produced by chance. It follows from this that only lines with a greater-than-chance proportion of points to length, say four or more to an alignment of ten miles (though the proportion is obviously dependent on the total number of points in any particular area) can be acceptable.

It is nevertheless the case, as worldwide records testify, that in antiquity the positions of buildings and the layout of areas were selected in a precisely determined manner in relation to pre-existent conditions: water supply, strategic importance, suitability of the ground for building, solar and lunar orientations,

Top, *the use of a baculum or Jacob's Staff is illustrated in an engraving of 1563. The instrument was employed from early times in surveying and navigation, and in China was known as a 'crossbow'.* Above, *a thirteenth-century astrolabe, one of the accurate measuring instruments available to medieval technicians.*

and, in the case of churches, their function in the hierarchy of ecclesiastical structures. Parishes were laid out with relation to each other, presupposing a geometrical system. Churches which superseded megalithic structures incorporated the astronomical alignments to points visible on the horizon.

Such alignments can also be seen and walked along. But whether the countryside is underlain with localized geometrical patterns, or whether they extend across unimaginable distances, construction of such patterns would require unified methodology and centralized control. Both of these have been demonstrated by Professor Thom to have been available in the megalithic period in Britain. Another problem raised by such alignments is the purpose of such constructions. Watkins believed they were trackways, and indeed, many of the alignments cited by him actually are used as tracks or roads to this day. Others seem never to have been used as tracks, which to some observers suggests they may have been part of a long-lost survey of the country by a vanished civilization. If they are instruments of a lost science, these remnants represent the implementation of an even greater level of control over the land than would have been countenanced in the days before the omphalos had been fixed. However, it appears that the laying out of the land by these invisible lines predates the foundation of cities, as it is these which eventually led to another reordering of the areas which became dependent upon them – the countryside.

Direction

7

A human being naturally sees the world in terms of his physical presence upon it, and, as a bilaterally symmetrical animal, he has four standard orientations or directions: in front, behind, left and right. These correspond microcosmically with the macrocosm of the earth upon which we live, which by its structure naturally presupposes four directions, defined by the two poles of the axis upon which it rotates, north and south, and the directions of the rising and setting sun – east and west.

Thus the 'natural' division into four of the field surrounding the individual corresponds directly with the observable phenomena of the earth, so it is not surprising that the concept of four directions forms a fundamental grounding in geomancy. Just as the individual, wherever he or she might be, is the centre of his or her experience, which is received with reference to four directions, so, in geomantic lore, the omphalos is the central reference point from which the four directions are viewed. In many cultures, these four directions were assigned a specific ritual colour, and the rulership of a spirit, regent, power, angel or god.

The simplest temple for the adoration of the gods is the human body itself, and the human body is indeed the frame of reference of the directions. Ancient Irish literature speaks of the east as 'in front', west as 'behind', north as 'left' and south as 'right'. These are the positions relative to the body of a worshipper facing the rising sun or, by later analogy, in an orientated church. In Hebrew, the same terminology applies, although Jewish synagogues are not usually orientated towards the east. The same scheme is preserved in Cambridge in the name given to a large area of trees and lawns beside the River Granta – the Backs. These are so called because they are to the west of the colleges of St John's, Trinity, Clare, King's, St Catharine's and Queens', and hence behind the backs of worshippers in their respective chapels.

This terminology appears to be based upon sacred orientation, the position adopted by the worshipper

The five directions, north, south, east, west, and centre: a Mixtec (Mexico) illustration dating from before 1350.

during devotional exercises. The secular orientation, in order that it might be distinguished from the sacred, was at right-angles from it. The Cambridge college halls preserve the ancient secular orientation, in which the lord or king and his courtiers would sit on a raised platform at the north end of the hall, facing southwards to dispense justice and largesse. At Cambridge, the Master and Fellows sit at the north end and face south. Scottish dialect preserves a memory of this secular orientation when it speaks of the 'east' or 'west' pocket of a coat, or of a postage stamp being at the top east corner of a letter. Here, the speaker or object is assumed to be facing north, the position of a commoner before the monarch. Such references to direction presumably originate from an archaic period before the formal finalizing of the points of the compass into north, south, east and west. They may be derived from lay or rustic usage where they survived unaltered.

The four directions are symbolic of the stability of the omphalos from which they originate. In turn, they must be guarded against attack from the powers of dissolution. In many ancient cosmologies, the directions therefore have guardians whose task is to ensure the safety of the omphalos. In the Persian *Avesta* the guardians are known as the Chieftains of the Four Sides; in Buddhist cosmology, likewise, they defend the world against demons.

The quaternary scheme of the world, according to a seventeenth-century diagram from west India. The expanding world is centred on the axis of Mount Meru.

Powers and colours traditionally associated with the four directions are found in the Judaeo-Christian tradition. The vision of Ezekiel, for instance, refers to a composite beast embodying the traditional Jewish guardians of the four directions. Another manifestation of the vision of Ezekiel are the four angels of Enoch: Michael, Raphael, Gabriel and Phanuel, whose cosmological function is identical as upholders of the central pivot of the universe, God. Perhaps the best-known of Biblical guardians are the Four Horsemen of the Apocalypse, which embody the colour code which is a characteristic of directional systems throughout the world. Zechariah saw four chariots which were drawn by red, black, white and grisled horses. The apocalyptic riders were mounted upon white, red, black and pale steeds. The colours of these powers of the four directions correspond remarkably with those of the native cultures of Central and North America. Three directional colours in the Mayan, Hopi and Oglala Sioux cosmologies are identical, and if 'pale' is interpreted as yellow, all four colours correspond.

The correspondence of these colours is a constant reminder of the unified system of magic, astronomy, astrology and topography, which was formerly integrated within a single practice. The Hebrew system is one of the most interesting, for it has survived cultural change to become the orthodox system in the Christian

Opposite, *the Four Horsemen of the Apocalypse, negative figures contrasting with the benevolent archangel-guardians of the four directions. Woodcut by Albrecht Dürer, 1498.*

Tantric Buddhist cosmogram of the central mountain of the world with the corresponding colours of the four directions.

religion. The four Evangelists of the Christian system reproduce the Ezekielan vision: St Mark is symbolized by the lion, St Luke by the bull, St Matthew by the angel or man, and St John by the eagle. These can most often be found engraved upon medieval coffin slabs or tomb canopies. A fine example is over the tomb of the Black Prince in Canterbury Cathedral, which doubly demonstrates their protective function. In this role they serve as the guardians of the four corners of the consecrated enclosure in which the corpse rests. Compare the nursery rhyme:

> *Matthew, Mark, Luke and John,*
> *Bless the bed that I lie on.*
> *Two to foot and two to head,*
> *Four to carry me when I'm dead.*

Here the four guardians are again enshrined. Their positioning thus not only ensures the correct orientation of the tombs of the dead, but even the beds of the living, as microcosms of the world with its quadripartite division.

In the Hindu religion, the quadripartite division originated at Mount Meru, the world's central omphalos.

The four rivers of the world sprang forth from this cosmological centre through the mouth of four symbolic animals. In China the symbolism was laid out in actual visible form at Peking in the Temple of the Spirits of the Land and Grain. Here the temple was constructed on an earthen terrace whose four sides were coloured according to the corresponding directions. The inner enclosing wall was also built in the brick of its special colour. In imitation, the Japanese Shinto temples often incorporated into their fabric the appropriate direction colours.

In early Mexico the god Tezcatlipoca was assigned a fivefold aspect, and this was later upgraded into five separate gods. Initially, he represented the centre and the four cardinal points surrounded by the four traditional colours. Later, the four variants of the one supreme god became differentiated. The blue of the south became Tlaloc, god of rain; the red east became Xipe Totec, sunrise; the north remained the domain of Tezcatlipoca himself, and the west was appropriated by the Plumed Serpent, Quetzalcoatl.

The major different colour systems of the world may be summarized in the following way, which demonstrates their fundamental variance.

	Centre	East	North	West	South
Aztec		red	white	black	blue
Chinese	yellow	blue	black	white	red
Irish		red	black	green	white
Hindu		white	brown	yellow	red
Maya/Hopi	blue-green	red	white	black	yellow
Tibetan	white	blue	green	red	yellow

Just as the four directions were ascribed their sacred correspondences, so the cosmological scheme of the four quarters of the earth served as the basis for both the geomantic design of cities and even the ideal scheme of whole countries. The concepts of the quadripartite division of the world and the corresponding guardians have appeared in almost all cultures.

Ancient Ireland was traditionally divided into four provinces, with Tara, seat of the high kings, at its geomantic centre, which completed the five directions as the meeting-point of the other four. At assemblies at Tara, the ritually determined positions of the different classes of society reproduced in microcosm the whole order of the nation. In this way, the centre stood for

kingship, the north was reserved for the warrior caste, the east for craftspeople, the south for musicians, and the west for the learned.

Iceland was likewise divided on cosmological lines. A quadripartite division of the whole island was in turn subdivided into twelve – three subdivisions for each quarter. At its geomantic centre was the Althing or parliament. When this was convened, a special place was reserved solely for it, and a temporary town was set up there which reproduced in microcosm the geomantic layout of the whole country and its social order. The Isle of Man still preserves such a ceremonial geomantic parliament with Tynwald Hill, which is composed of soil taken from the seventeen parishes of the Isle. Constructed, like many a holy mountain, in tiers, the hill is a microcosm of the hierarchy of Manx government. At the Tynwald ceremony, the governor and council occupy the topmost tier, the members of the House of Keys the second, and the clergy the third.

The cult background of this artificial holy hill and its festival is demonstrated by the date of the annual ceremony – Midsummer Day. It serves to remind us that these assemblies were held not only in special places, but also at special times of year which bore significant relationships with the life of the agricultural community. Similar holy hills were used for conventions in many parts of Britain, each being the administrative omphalos of the district it represented. Their position is emphasized by their situation at the junction of several boundaries, especially the trifinion

The three-tiered Tynwald Hill, site of the Manx parliament, the House of Keys, is composed of soil from each of the parishes of the Isle of Man, and thus represents a microcosm of the whole island.

97

or meeting-place of three separate areas. These subdivisions, unlike the quadripartite division of the whole country, were into threes. The three Ridings of Yorkshire or the three divisions of Lincolnshire – Lindsey, Kesteven and Holland – are two examples which readily spring to mind.

Thus where the country was initially divided into four, each of the smaller zones were divided into three, making twelve in all. With the central omphalos, which was special and not included in the normal reckoning, the number of division is thirteen. A twelvefold division conveniently represents the totality of the year, moving around the central pivot, and this is a number which seems to hold an unusually powerful attraction for mankind. The day is divided into twelve hours, the calendar into twelve months, and the Hellenic zodiac into twelve signs. The Jewish nation had twelve tribes, a fact which was reflected in the number of Christ's apostles. Odysseus, Conchobar, Odin, Hrolf, Christ and Charlemagne all represent the focal point of twelve followers. In total, the number of each group is thirteen. The unluckiness of this number, which as the summation, the complete quota, should logically be the perfect number rather than an inauspicious one, may be explained by the necessity for it to occur only in the correct place, such as at the Manx Tynwald. To make up the number elsewhere may have been thought to generate powers which could not be brought under control without a cosmologically ordered layout, and thus to lead potentially to disaster. Such matters are now little understood, and fear of the number thirteen has become a superstition – something which 'stands over' from a former age. The place of such ritual in our society has been almost totally obliterated, and now is only preserved in superstition, tradition, and (to those with eyes to see) in the actual layout and design of many buildings and even cities.

Astronomical structure
Many of the world's famous sacred structures have recently been the subject of reappraisal in the light of the new subject of astro-archaeology. They have often been found to incorporate in their fabric and design a number of significant solar, lunar or even stellar orientations. It has been suggested that sacred buildings were often sited on an astronomical line with distant natural features as markers, and where these were absent, artificial foresights were laid out on the alignments in their stead.

Such observatory temples had a twofold function. First, they were centres of worship, the places where the prescribed rituals of the religion were enacted in order to gain favours, enhance harvests or blight enemies. Secondly, the temple itself was an instrument of astronomical observation and record. It indicated the equinoxes and solstices, which were used for checking and verifying the calendar. Other functions were often incorporated, making it possible for the astronomer priests to calculate the times of eclipses, the positions and times of moon and sunrise, and the measure of time throughout the day in an era before the invention of mechanical clocks.

Although Stonehenge's geometrical relationship with the heavens has already been discussed, its position in relation to other comparable sites in Britain is worth consideration. Stonehenge is a major factor in the geomantic alignments of southern Britain. It is on alignments which have been found to run from Glastonbury Abbey (E–W), and Salisbury Cathedral (N–S), which are of course important (Christianized) geomantic centres. Professor Thom has recently found that, in addition to its astronomical alignments, Stonehenge is constructed so that its inner 'circle' is one of the most exact megalithic ellipses on record. Several researchers, including Keith Critchlow and John Michell, have drawn attention to another curious coincidence at Stonehenge. According to their calculations, the underlying geometry and dimensions of the henge have an exact parallel in St Mary's Chapel at Glastonbury, which is the reputed site of the earliest Christian chapel.

Such complex and overlapping astronomical and geometrical functions must have been determined with minute accuracy. Technicians of a high order of competence, working within a nationwide framework, would have been necessary to fulfil all the conditions which can be ascertained from a close study of the various aspects of the siting and construction of Stonehenge.

Temples sited so as to indicate various important positions of the sun and moon may be found in all continents, but a particularly fine example of such geomantic siting and symbolic architecture is the Hindu cosmic shrine of Angkor Wat, Cambodia. Originally dedicated to the worship of the deity Vishnu, the temple complex was built during the reign of the Khmer King Suryavarman II, (AD 1113–c. 1150). The temple consists of five massive concentric

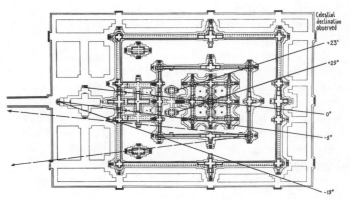

The great Hindu temple of Angkor Wat, Cambodia. In addition to being designed as an expression of sacred history, the actual position of the whole temple is related to sighting points on the horizon (see ground plan), and its façades and towers are arranged to enable it to function as a celestial observatory.

rectangular orientated enclosures extending for 1650 yards from east to west and 1430 yards from north to south – a remarkable feat of engineering.

The enclosure is entered by a bridge over a wide moat designed to exclude malevolent powers, and the way goes on through the main entrance gate. Immediately inside the gate is a causeway 382 yards long which leads in a straight line to the sanctuary. This is placed directly above the omphalos, which is marked by the tallest and central of a cluster of five towers. The whole structure is orientated in such a way that the profile of the western entrance gateway complex marks the significant positions of the sun and moon when viewed from the central towers. In all, 22 major positions of sun and moon are marked in this way, a system which forms a direct parallel with that found at Stonehenge and other megalithic observatories. Angkor Wat, moreover, is constructed according to the foursquare design of the 'holy city' – the quadripartite division of the earth which is repeated in temples and cities in all continents.

The Big Horn Medicine Wheel, Wyoming USA, photographed in 1926 when it was protected by a stone wall. The Wheel's 28 spokes correspond with the 28 struts in the Oglala Sioux Medicine lodge and carefully sited cairns indicate important star-rise positions (see p. 119).

We know that North America once possessed numerous mounds, animal effigies and geometrical enclosures constructed by the native tribes. Of these structures one at least, the stone 'wheel' known as the Big Horn Medicine Wheel, is an outstanding example of a design determined by astronomical alignments. Situated at an altitude of 9700 feet on a shoulder of the sacred Medicine Mountain in the Big Horn Mountains, northern Wyoming, the wheel is a pattern of large stones laid in an imperfect circle of *c.* 82 feet diameter. At the centre of the circle is a cairn about 12 feet in diameter. From this central cairn radiate 28 unevenly spaced lines of stones, the spokes which connect with the rim of the wheel. Five smaller cairns, each an open circle about three feet in diameter, are placed at irregular intervals on the rim.

Comparable structures known to have been erected by native Americans are the Medicine lodges of the Cheyenne tribe and the Sun Dance lodges of the Oglala Sioux. These were orientated structures set up at particular times for the performance of special religious rituals. John Eddy surveyed the Big Horn Medicine Wheel, which has been dated by tree-ring evidence to the eighteenth century of our era. He discovered that the various cairns on the wheel's periphery were, like the foresights and backsights at Stonehenge (and the western gateway at Angkor Wat), eight markers for solstitial sunrises and sunsets. In addition, they marked the rising of the three most important stars: Rigel in Orion, Aldebaran in Taurus, and Sirius in Canis Major.

Although it could equally well have been constructed on the nearby plains, the Medicine Wheel was placed on an inaccessible holy mountain. Here, it was used for calendric purposes. Aldebaran's helical rising at solstice time was known and used in the calendars of the Central American and Hopi nations, and it may be

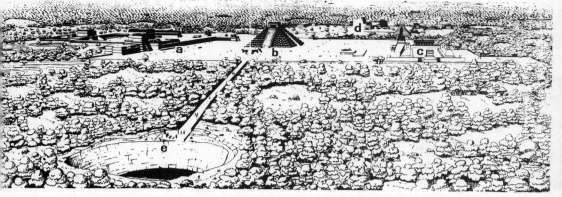

inferred that this cultural trait existed in the tribes who constructed the wheel. The accuracy of astronomical alignments at the Big Horn Medicine Wheel may be seen as a northern manifestation of the better-known astronomical architecture of the Central American Maya, whose complex astronomical observatory at Chichen Itza (the Caracol) is perhaps the most celebrated. These, however, are perhaps nearer in spirit to Angkor Wat than to Medicine Mountain. The Caracol, a circular tower now partially in ruins, possesses various windows and apertures on significant orientations of sunrise and star-rise. Being in the centre of a temple complex, its function cannot be separated from the rituals of the priests who were trained to observe the heavens.

Chichen Itza, Mexico, an important Mayan ceremonial centre. A causeway linked the major pyramid (b) with the Cenote (e), a well into which sacrificial objects and people were thrown. The site also included the Caracol (d), a circular building with windows acting as sighting apertures.

Specific sun orientations

Orientation of whole buildings towards a specific sunrise is common in many ancient sanctuaries. For example, many megalithic burial barrows such as Coldrum in Kent, West Kennet in Wiltshire, and New Grange in Ireland, are orientated towards sunrise. New Grange, the most famous Irish neolithic passage grave, which dates from around 3100 BC, was as recently as 1972 found to possess an unusual structure above the entrance, a 'roof-box' (as it has been called) which was studied by Professor M. O'Kelly. He found that it was placed precisely to project a ray of sunlight only at midwinter sunrise onto the triple spiral figure in the rear recess of the burial chamber, more than 60 feet inside. The construction of the burial mound was therefore determined by the orientation of midwinter sunrise at New Grange, its axis ascertained by direct observation.

At Abu Simbel in Egypt the rock-cut temples were similarly orientated, so that twice a year the sun would

shine directly upon the faces of the images of Rameses II, Amon-Re and Re-Harakhty. This temple, which had been quarried out of the solid rock, was threatened with destruction by the rising waters of the new Aswan dam, but UNESCO raised the necessary money to demolish and re-erect it above the new waterline. The engineers took care to reproduce the orientation exactly so that, although the temple has been demolished and re-erected, the images of the king and his guardian gods are still illuminated as of old.

Abu Simbel is only one of many early temples in which the image of the god or goddess was illuminated by the sun's rays at a predetermined time. The projection of a ray of sunlight on a specific day of the year ensured that the image received the light only at the time selected by the orientation of the building. Such special times, generally equinoxes or solstices, but sometimes patronal days, reproduced the astrological conditions prevailing at the time of dedication, special and unique conditions for the performance of whatever ritual or process was desired.

Mithras, the Persian god worshipped by soldiers throughout the Roman empire, was a solar deity, but he was worshipped in shrines which were almost invariably subterranean. In keeping with his solar role, however, the sanctuary of the god was so arranged that a shaft of sunlight would illuminate the image of the god at sunrise. Although Mithraea were wantonly destroyed by the Christians when their religion was officially recognized by the empire, many Christian churches were subsequently furnished with comparable features.

At Chartres Cathedral, a ray of white light issues from a piece of specially positioned plain glass in the stained-glass window of Saint Apollinaire. It is hard not to see this as a pagan survival of Apollo, since this spot of light may be seen to fall, at noon local time on 21 June, Midsummer Day, upon a special mark set in the floor to indicate the event. Such a solstitial mark in a Christian sanctuary is obviously not merely the product of the whim of an idle glazier, because complex calculations and direct observation would have been required to set up such a device. Similar arrangements still exist in the church of St Sulpice in Paris, Florence Cathedral, and the church of St Petronius in Bologna. These represent the remnants of a former widespread practice rather than isolated instances. A gnomon of more complex form, derived from earlier devices, was set up by Dom Camille Ferouillat at the Hospital of

Temples of celestial illumination: opposite (above), *the entrance to New Grange, the Irish megalithic tomb, is blocked by a spiral-marked entrance stone possibly corresponding to the spirit walls of Chinese temples, above which is the so-called 'roof-box', sited to catch a ray of light at midwinter sunrise, c. 3100* B C. Opposite (below), *the great Egyptian temple of Abu Simbel, where on a special day the sunlight penetrates the deepest recesses of the temple and illuminates the images of the tutelary gods.* Above, *the temple of Mithras, directly below the church of San Clemente, Rome, where a ray of light, entering its subterranean precincts, emphasized the solar mysteries to the devotees.*

Tonnerre as late as 1786, shortly before the French Revolution brought such matters to an abrupt close. There, a luminous spot is projected in the manner of Chartres from a window onto a lemniscate-shaped (figure of eight) brass strip set into the floor. The spot of light touches the strip precisely at midday.

These devices had a purely functional role as means of enabling the clergy to hold services at the correct time, but they also represent remnants of the ancient technique of determining orientation, for sundials, gnomons, and other orientation devices are all based on interrelated principles. Their direction or shadows are closely related to solar and geographical phenomena, and hence are of particular concern to geomancers. Some methods were derived from the construction of sundials, using techniques of direct observation.

In ancient Egypt the method of obtaining the desired orientation of the axis of a temple is recorded as having been determined by direct observation and measurement. This was carried out during the foundation ceremony known as *Pedjeshes* (Stretching the Cord). The ceremony is recorded in the major monumental inscriptions in the temples of Abydos, Denderah, Edfu and Heliopolis. The reigning king and a priestess representing Seshat, the goddess of writing, arrived on the site, each carrying a golden mallet and a cord with a peg at the ends. After some preliminary magical ritual, the priestess drove home her peg on the omphalos, while the king aligned the cord to the celestial object under observation, and fixed the peg into the ground. This established the orientation of the future temple, relating it directly to the position of the celestial object at the time of its foundation.

The orientation of Christian buildings
The English word orientation comes from the classical Latin word *oriri*, to rise. In the specific case, it refers to sunrise. Linguists have conjectured that the present English word might be derived from a medieval Latin verb *orientare*, which had the particular meaning of setting something towards the east. In medieval legend, Christ was believed to have been crucified with his back to the *compas*, the omphalos of Jerusalem, cosmological centre of the world, so it was deemed natural for worshippers in church to take up the stance of observers at the Crucifixion with their faces towards the cross. Christian churches were also built as microcosmic reproductions of the world, and therefore were generally orientated east-west, symbolizing the passage

of the sun each day through the world. However, the rule was not rigidly observed.

The general principle of the orientation of ancient Roman temples was set out by Vitruvius, an architectural theorist at the time of Augustus, in his highly influential *Ten Books on Architecture* (Bk IV, Ch. V):

The quarter towards which temples of the immortal gods ought to face is to be determined on the principle that, if there is no reason to hinder and the choice is free, the temple and the statue placed in the *cella* should face the western quarter of the sky. This will enable those who approach the altar with offerings or sacrifices to face the direction of sunrise in looking towards the statue of the temple, and thus those who are undertaking vows will look towards the quarter from whence the sun comes forth.

Vitruvian principles were in general followed by the Christians. One notable exception, however, is St Peter's in Rome, which faces west. But of course St Peter's, as the mother church of the Roman Catholic faith, is an important omphalos in itself, which naturally has less need of orientation towards some other point. The present Renaissance building is not the original, but replaced an ancient church of the imperial period which also had a westerly aspect, the reverse of the contemporary pagan temples. This orientation is alluded to in an edict, issued by Pope Leo I in AD 443, which condemned the general practice among the people of standing each morning on the steps at the eastern entry court of St Peter's to bow to the rising sun. Thirty years later, the *Apostolic Constitutions* of 472 ordained that churches were to be built according to a rectangular plan with the 'head' to the east. The congregation were literally directed to pray eastwards, which fixed the orientation until the rule was defied at the Reformation.

If one measures the angles of orientation of a number of churches, however, it will soon be noticed that few are accurately aligned towards true east, considerable variation being the rule. Indeed, Salisbury Cathedral, begun in 1220, is unusual because it is aligned exactly between the equinoctial sunrise and sunset. Records of the techniques employed in determining the orientation of churches show that most were sited according to the apparent position of sunrise on the day dedicated to the patronal saint. Thus a St George's church ought to be aligned on sunrise of 23 April; a St Stephen's church on that of 26 December, and so on. Perhaps the earliest written evidence for this comes through Silas Taylor (alias Domville), a captain in the Parliamentary army during the English Civil War, who commanded a unit which ransacked the cathedral libraries at Hereford and Worcester. It is likely that Taylor carried away whatever ancient manuscripts took his fancy.

After the war he took up antiquarian studies, and one of his manuscripts contains the following extract, probably derived from ancient documents:

In the days of yore, when a church was to be built, they watched and prayed on the vigil of the dedication, and took that point of the horizon where the sun rose in the east, which makes that variation, so that few stand true, except those built between the equinoxes [i.e. in axial terms]. I have experimented some churches and have found the line to point to that part of the horizon where the sun arises on the day of the saint to whom the church is dedicated.

Traditions still extant in Scottish Freemasonry record the same procedure. W. A. Laurie, in *The History of Free Masonry and the Grand Lodge of Scotland* (1859), wrote as follows:

On the evening previous, the Patrons, Ecclesiastics and Masons assembled and spent the night in devotional exercises: one being placed to watch the rising of the sun, gave notice when his rays appeared above the horizon. When fully in view, the Master Mason sent out a man with a rod, which he ranged in line between the altar and the sun, and thus fixed a line of orientation.

The tomb shrine of King Edward the Confessor in Westminster Abbey, Built over a powerful 'blind spring', the shrine illustrates the geomancers' concern with precise orientation.

This record is particularly interesting in that it specifies the sun being in full view, i.e. the whole disc being above the horizon, which has been a bone of contention in the astro-archaeologists' analysis of the positions of sunrise markers.

Grave orientation often enables archaeologists to identify an area of Christian interment. The orientation arises from the Christian belief that the Second Coming of Christ would originate in the east. The antiquity of the practice is well established, and even in an age when churches are no longer specially sited, grave orientation is still often carried out. The belief that the correct positioning of the burial sites of the dead affords good fortune either to the spirits of the deceased or his descendants appears as a constant theme in all cultures. It is especially emphasized in Chinese Feng-Shui, in the siting of English royal tombs, and in the burial of national leaders, even such recent figures as Napoleon I and Generalissimo Franco (see p. 168). Orientation ensures integration of the dead with the cosmos, thus avoiding the dangers of an unquiet grave.

In the 1950s, the Rev. Hugh Benson compared the evidence of several writers with the actual orientation of churches in relation to their dedicatory saints and sunrise alignments. Basing his work upon churches in Oxfordshire, he demonstrated that most were orientated on the sunrise of important church festivals, after taking into account the changes in the calendar and changes in patronal dedications. He cleared up the problem of several 'inaccurate' patronal orientations of buildings in hilly or built-up districts by pointing out that there was no anomaly – the builders merely observed the actual position of sunrise over nearby hills or buildings. This proved to be correct at Cambridge, where King's College Chapel was constructed in an already built-up area, and the orientation for the patronal day was modified accordingly. This pragmatic method should not seem surprising, as it is identical with that employed at megalithic sites 3,000 years before, viewing the actual rather than the theoretical sunrise. Only people no longer in touch with the natural world, like ourselves, would try to use theoretical rather than observable phenomena as a base for action.

In addition to orientation by means of the sun, it has long been surmised that the magnetic compass may have been used to determine the orientation of certain ancient sacred buildings. It was proposed as early as 1906 by H. Wehner that the magnetic compass was used by the medieval Freemasons, but the best evidence yet advanced for a limited usage has recently been put forward by Sidney Searle. The magnetism of the earth (unlike the true axis of spin), is a variable field whose poles wander within ill-defined areas close to the axial poles. Magnetic variations, (i.e. the angular differences between true north and magnetic north from any point on the earth's surface), has varied through the centuries. For 400 years, ever since its discovery in the West by Stephen Burrowes (1525–1584) on a voyage made in 1553, its changes have been documented. Complete records have been kept since the variation was calculated by Doctor Gillebrand, professor of geometry at Gresham College, Oxford, a contemporary of Burrowes.

Modern science has revealed that the recurrence of heating and re-heating of pottery kilns causes them to retain the magnetic field direction of the time they were last in use. This knowledge has enabled scientists to compare the magnetic directions in kilns of known age with others of unknown age, and thus to build up a magnetic field chronology. The science of archaeomagnetism, as it is called, has enabled us to construct a chart of the variations in magnetic north for over a millennium before the direct records of Burrowes and his successors. Correlation of dates can be adduced by comparison with the data available from the ancient Chinese geomancers.

Sidney Searle studied the orientation of a number of churches, including Chichester Cathedral, and noticed a correlation between their angle of orientation and their dates of construction. In the church of Bosham, Sussex, where the orientation of part of the building dated from the Roman period, AD 340, the bases of the columns of a Roman basilica which had predated the church were found to be still in situ. These were orientated 6° north of east, correct for a magnetic variation from true north in AD 340. Other parts of the church also have the correct orientations for the magnetic variation at their respective historical periods. This variation in the orientation of different parts of the same building has been proposed as a solution to the knotty problem of the so-called 'deflected chancel', where the nave and chancel of a church are out of alignment. Solutions to this problem vary from the absurd suggestion that the builders were incompetent, even at cathedrals which have stood for centuries, to the hypothesis that, since the church was symbolic of the body of Christ, the chancel's deflection represented Christ's head rolling over to one side when on the cross. Searle claimed that the different parts of the church were built at different times and, as they were orientated by the magnetic compass, their alignments would differ with the wandering of the magnetic pole. The masons, being schooled in an art which was directly related to the earth, would not defy the compass since it registered an actual, rather than a theoretical, flow of current – the magnetic field of the earth.

A possible reconciliation of the seemingly contradictory evidence of Benson and Searle may be that both methods were used in parallel, perhaps practised by two separate schools of geomancers. They may even have had subtly differing purposes whose knowledge is now lost. Evidence for the use of the compass is only circumstantial in the West, though in 1735 the antiquary Thomas Hearne ordered that a compass should be used to determine the correct orientation of his grave. This may have been the tail end of a Western geomantic tradition. In ancient China, the magnetic compass was an essential tool employed by geomancers, and its use in geomancy predated by centuries its use in navigation. Geomancers used the compass to

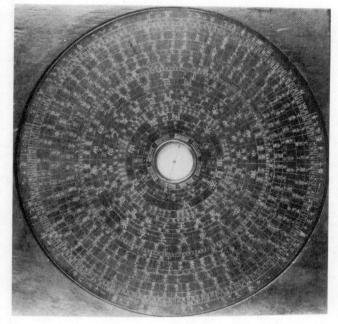

A Chinese geomancer's compass, representative of the technical branch of the subject. Each ring around the magnetic needle is compared with the observed features of the landscape, the auspices to be determined, and the action to be taken. The three circles, which relate to the secular variation of the compass in the eighth, ninth and twelfth centuries A D, have become 'fossilized' in the system.

determine the orientation of tombs, temples and secular buildings, and the alignments of city walls and streets.

The Chinese geomancer's compass is a complex instrument which was developed over the centuries to enable the practitioner to make precise calculations in the subtle art of Feng-Shui. Owing to continuous alterations in magnetic variation, three systems superimposed one upon another became institutionalized in the standard compass which practitioners of Feng-Shui use today.

These three variant orientations evolved over a period of 500 years. The true terrestrial north-south meridian was first set down by Chhiu Yen-Han (*c.* A D 713–41), and was known as the *chêng chan*. It remained in use as the sole graduation on compasses until about A D 880, when the variation had become so pronounced that a new graduation became an urgent necessity. The geomancer Yang Yün-Sung added a staggered system of points to the compass to compensate for the variation. Known as the 'seam needle' or *fêng chen*, this circle of points was $7\frac{1}{2}°$ to the west of the *chêng chen*, as the earth's magnetic pole had shifted to the east of true north. By the twelfth century A D, even this system was no longer usable, as the pole had now shifted westwards and another recalibration of the compass was needed. The third system, instituted by the geomancer Lai Wen-Chün, was termed *chung chen* (the

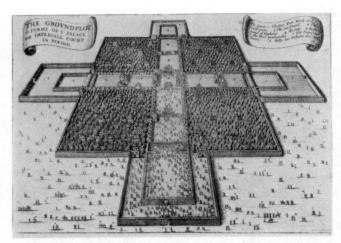

The Forbidden City of Peking, the most sacred part of pre-Communist China, was laid out on the principle of a cross superimposed on a square.

central needle), and consisted of yet another circle of graduations, this time $7\frac{1}{2}°$ east of the meridional line.

These attempts to come to terms with what is essentially an irregularly variable phenomenon, the secular variation of the compass needle, led the Chinese to produce architecture with the same variation in orientation as we have seen in Europe. The walls of Peking, a cosmologically designed city whose orientation should be true north-south, are in reality $2\frac{1}{2}°$ out of meridian to the west, a magnetic variation which correlates with the year of their construction – AD 1410. Divergent orientations of 11° exist in the street grids of Shantan in Kansu province, and, though the southern part of Nanking is aligned to true north-south, the walls and most streets are orientated 13° to the east of them. In an unconscious way, these variant orientations reproduce the conditions of terrestrial magnetism which prevailed at the time of their foundation.

The occurrence of divergent orientations in temporarily separate structures is not restricted to the Old World. John B. Carlson of Maryland University has detected the same phenomenon in Olmec ceremonial sites at La Venta, Tabasco, in Mexico. Many Olmec sites possess an orientation of 8° west of true north, e.g. those at La Venta, Laguna de los Cerros and Huitzo, Oaxaca. Like many other ancient cultures, the Olmec priesthood designed buildings for ritual use where orientation played an important role. The orientation of the whole San Lorenzo plateau, which was artificially modified to make it animal-shaped, is to azimuthal north-south. Carlson's team successfully predicted the sites of buried ceremonial caches along the central axis, which led him to speculate on the similarity of the geomantic positioning of sites in Mexico with those in

China. One of the ceremonial caches contained the clue: a highly polished bar of haematite with a trapezoid cross-section was discovered which, when examined by the archaeologist M. D. Coe, was found to be capable of functioning as a lodestone floater compass, as it was magnetized in that way. Integration of the observed facts, the geomantic practices of the Olmecs, and the deviation from true north, led Carlson to claim that the item found was part of a geomancer's compass, the first to be discovered in the Americas.

These possible uses of the magnetic compass in geomancy long before its application to navigation suggest that its properties were regarded as an important mystery to be kept from the scrutiny of the uninitiated. All over the world, small élite groups of initiates have been the recipients of complex technical knowledge and expertise, from the early calendar-makers of antiquity to the nuclear physicists of today. Nowadays, the concept of arcane secrets is outmoded, but there are nevertheless many skills requiring specialized knowledge and expert instruction, from flying an aeroplane to operating an electron micro-scope. Unpublicized and unpublished knowledge in an age of mass ignorance could have been kept secret without much difficulty. Admission to an order requiring silence as the price of admission, enforced perhaps by the threat of the death penalty, may have been the only way that a man might obtain such knowledge. The Horseman's Oath (that of a Scottish secret society) and, of course, the Freemason's Oath, both threaten dire penalties for divulging the secrets to non-members; perhaps the compass was kept secret in China by such methods, and it is possible that its application to navigation was an independent dis-covery. But once known, the mystique of the geomancer's magnetic compass was much diminished.

Renaissance and post-Renaissance church orientation
At the time of the Reformation in England, certain zealots deliberately altered the traditional orientation of churches. At Cambridge in 1584, Sir Walter Mildmay, a Puritan extremist, took over a range of buildings which had formerly composed the local Dominican priory. This had been suppressed in 1536, and its buildings were considered ideal for the foundation of a new college for the instruction of Protestant clerics. Wishing to break with what he considered 'popish' practice, Mildmay converted the priory's refectory, which was aligned north-south, into the chapel. The

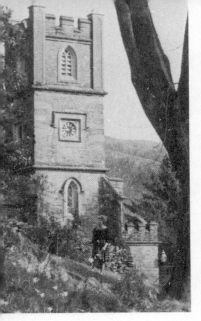

Rydal Chapel in Westmoreland (Cumbria), whose foundation in 1823 according to ancient geomantic usage is recorded in Wordsworth's poem, 'On seeing the foundation prepared for Rydal Chapel'.

former Dominican chapel, orientated east-west, was profaned by conversion into the hall of the new Emmanuel College.

This move was greatly criticized at the time, as Mildmay had moved the place of worship from the omphalos to a non-sacred site as well as defying ancient practice. But Puritans like the diarist Evelyn, who referred to Emmanuel College as 'that zealous house, reformed *ab origine*', tended to approve. In altering the orientation, Mildmay was following the example of certain Puritan preachers who chose to hold their services in St Paul's Cathedral at a tomb on the north side rather than to use the high altar at the east end.

Some 30 years later, King James I visited Cambridge. When his attention was drawn to the incorrect orientation of the chapel, he remarked, 'God would not turn away His face from the prayers of any holy and pious man to whatever region of the heavens he directs his eyes'. This reveals a typically Protestant viewpoint, indicating a strong rejection of any belief in the efficacy of geomantic practices.

However, Emmanuel College Chapel was never properly consecrated. A century after its 'reformation *ab origine*', a new chapel was erected to the designs of Sir Christopher Wren. Orientated about 30° to the north of east, it seems that the alignment was none too carefully measured, although highly accurate surveying instruments were available.

Later church building in England was sparse until the Wesleyan revival, when chapels were constructed, like the Quaker counterparts, with little regard to orientation. We can, of course, find some exceptions which prove the rule of disorientation. Rydal Chapel, for example, was founded with full masonic form. It appears that an understanding of geomantic orientation as a factor in church architecture was clear to only a few of the many church architects who flourished in the Victorian Anglican renaissance. In most cases, spiritual considerations were relegated to second place behind financial requirements. The choice of site was determined by availability of land, and the existing orientation of the streets usually fixed the axial alignment.

However, mystic proportional systems were certainly used by some architects. The Victorian church of St George, Tufnell Park in north London, now converted into a theatre, was constructed exactly according to the dimensions of the fifth-century octagonal church of St George's, Thessaloniki.

Latter-day deviations from the east are numerous, but we may single out the curious case of St George's church, Bloomsbury, London. This was designed by Wren's follower Hawksmoor, and was orientated in the normal manner until the local landowner, the Duke of Bedford, presented it with an altarpiece which was too wide for the main axis. But the gift was too good to be refused, and it was placed in the north transept along with the altar, which effectively slewed the church's axis by 90°. Nobody seems to have thought anything unusual in the procedure. The modern Anglican cathedrals at Liverpool and Coventry are no better. They are both orientated north-south, that at Coventry being obviously at right-angles to the old building which was smashed in 1941.

Finally, the nineteenth century furnishes us with two examples which demonstrate two almost diametrically opposed reasons for the use of orientation in new buildings. In the early nineteenth century, a controversy arose over the orientation of new Christian churches in India, which were to be built under the aegis of Dr Middleton, the first bishop of Calcutta (1814–22). It was argued that churches ought to face towards Jerusalem in the same way that mosques face towards Mecca, and in India this would of course make for a westerly orientation. On the other hand, it was pointed out that orientated churches in England face Moscow rather than Jerusalem, and since churches traditionally face the east, this was done in India. But the rising sun was not mentioned, for this would have admitted a pagan element into the controversy.

When the American writer Henry Thoreau constructed his cabin at Walden Pond, he orientated its diagonal towards the equinoctial sunrise in order that he might be in harmony with nature. Whether this was done as the result of ancient tradition or personal belief is not known.

Today, only the Islamic religion takes great care to orientate its sacred buildings, keeping its mosques towards Mecca, the Holy City. Christian architecture no longer makes any pretence of integration with the created world. The geometrical shapes used are employed for their aesthetic and engineering qualities, which are now taken in isolation, and no longer fulfil their earlier rôle of forming an integral part of the link between humanity and the cosmos.

Interior of St George's church, Salonika, Greece, a fifth-century Byzantine round church whose geometry was based on the circle and the octagon. The nineteenth-century church of St George's, Tufnell Park, London, follows the same scheme.

8 Sacred geometry

He took the golden compasses, prepar'd
In God's eternal store, to circumscribe
This Universe, and all created things:
One foot he center'd, and the other turn'd
Round through the vast profunditie obscure,
And said, thus farr extend, thus farr thy bounds,
Thus be thy just circumference, O world.

John Milton, *Paradise Lost*.

Shapes and patterns have a basic significance for all animals which possess the faculty of vision; for the human race, these patterns are doubly potent as they also have deeply rooted psychological meanings. It is very easy, perhaps deceptively so, to use the ideas of the pioneer psychologist Jung and his followers to explain the source of all geomantic images in terms of internal structures and archetypes. To do this requires a considerably more sophisticated knowledge of the internal and external worlds than we at present possess. However, as a working model it has its merits.

Archetypes are the images which have been observed by psychologists to be repeatedly and spontaneously generated by the psyche. The psychological counterparts of instincts, archetypal patterns represent inherent conceptual images of the unconscious mind which occur in dreams and visions. According to this theory, 'magic' images are symbolic analogies directly affecting the unconscious mind, which can only be touched or even expressed by reference to the symbol. Hence, imagery which is found to express universally constant themes may be directly related to archetypal patterns of the mind. If it is borne in mind that Jung's ideas are working tools rather than objective truth, they can be profitably applied to the subject under discussion.

Geometry literally means 'measuring the earth'. It is the basis of all architecture. Without geometry, there could be no calculation, no design. It is fundamental to the measurement of area and the estimation of volume. Above all, it is richly symbolic, both on the archetypal and intellectual levels. Geometry is fundamental; it is universal. The structure of things, both organic and inorganic, is based upon the universal rules of

The medieval European vision of God as Great Architect of the Universe, measuring the cosmos with the traditional compass – fundamental tool of geometer and mason.

Inspired by the neolithic monuments of Avebury, William Blake's allegorical illustration, The Serpent Temple, *links the masonic tradition of compass-wielding Creator with the solar and lunar attributes of megalithic sites.*

geometry. Through geometry, the living and the non-living, the natural and the artificial, are linked with the various material, psychological and spiritual planes which constitute the basis of religious experience. Geometry is the symbolic code which enabled geometricians and geomancers to infuse their work with the arcane mysteries, and provided the builders with the means of applying a numerical, numerological and metrological system to their temples.

In classical Euclidean geometry, the only instruments permitted the student are straight-edge and compasses, but these are quite sufficient for drawing a number of important figures: the circle, the vesica piscis, the triangle, the square, the pentagram and the pentagon. All may be produced quite simply without recourse to measurement, and they all display proportional ratios which are pleasing to the eye and promote a feeling of well-being in the beholder. The most celebrated of these is the *sectio divina* or Golden Section. The ground plans and elevations of the great religious buildings of the world were generated from such geometrical figures. Regardless of religion, the archetypal images of geometry permeate sacred architecture, their forms transcending sectarianism and reflecting a higher truth.

The geometrical basis of the temple is deliberately designed as a microcosmic image of universal order, acting as a catalyst which enables the individual to harmonize with the cosmos. Hence the temple itself must be an accurate reflection of the cosmos, and be in harmony with it. The *Manasara-Shilpa Shastra*, a Hindu Sanskrit text on the layout of temples, demonstrates this fundamental integration of sacred geometry with site and orientation. The document records the initial processes of founding the temple, whose basic plan is derived from the geometry required to procure orientation. This process is a rite in the proper sense of the word, for it connects the actual form of the temple with that of the universe, which in this case is seen as the expression of the divine power. A pillar was set up in the place chosen for the building of the temple, and a circle was drawn around it. The pillar served as a gnomon, whose shadow-lines at dawn and dusk were marked off on the circle, giving a true east–west axis. These two points were taken as centres for marking out two circles which intersect to give a vesica. A line drawn between the vertices of the vesica gave the north-south axis. The intersections of other circles, centred on the four ends of the axes, afforded the means

Christ enclosed in a vesica, at the centre of the four guardian animals of the Evangelists. From the Royal Portal of Chartres Cathedral.

of establishing the four corners of a square, which was orientated to the true cardinal points. The square is thus the quadrature of the solar cycle of which the circle around the original gnomon is the direct representation.

This fundamental figure, the vesica piscis, is the practical point of departure from which all geometrical figures may be derived. In psychological terms, this fundamental nature was manifested as a symbol of perceived knowledge and perpetual attention.

From the vesica, the equilateral triangle may be derived by the simple expedient of dividing the vesica across its length and connecting each end of the line thus produced to each vertex. Two equal equilateral triangles base to base are thus made. The production of the square has been described above. Precise geometrical relationships between lengths and proportion are thus produced naturally, repeating proportions found throughout the natural world, and so reinforcing the feeling of continuity with the created macrocosm.

The circle

One of the most ancient of the symbols used by humanity, the circle, is also perhaps the easiest to draw. It is seen each day in the form of the disc of the sun, and occurs naturally in the mineral, plant and animal kingdoms. Early wooden buildings were invariably circular on a basic pattern which can be still encountered in different forms all over the world today. The circular form of a hut, yurt or tipi inherently echoes the circle of the horizon, the ceiling representing the sky. This obvious parallel with the world becomes explicit in sacred architecture, the circle being seen as an embodiment of the universal whole, representing perfection and completeness.

Although the circular building has come down to recent times as a theme in both Christian and oriental sacred architecture, we must look to the native tribes of North America for the purest and most explicit manifestation of the ultimate purpose of such structures. Black Elk, the Oglala Sioux holy man, has made a record of his people's sacred knowledge, despite his great age and the suffering inflicted upon his people by the whites. According to this source, one of the many ceremonies of the sacred year of the Oglala Sioux was the setting up of the Sun Dance lodge. First, the holy man would go out with his helper to find the sacred rustling cottonwood tree which was to be the central support for the lodge, and having selected it, to mark it

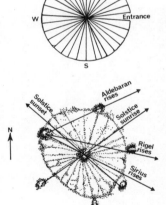

The Oglala Sioux Medicine lodges had 28 spokes radiating from the central omphalos pole, representing the days of the lunar month. This 28-fold division of the circle was reproduced in the Big Horn Medicine Wheel (bottom) *whose cairns indicate important star-rise positions on the horizon.*

One of the few round churches to retain its central altar: St Michael's at Fulda, W. Germany.

with sage. Next day the holy man offered his pipe to the tree and told it that it had been chosen in a sacred manner to stand at the centre of the sacred hoop, the crossing of the four sacred paths, the centre of the great powers of the universe. After offering his pipe to heaven and earth, the holy man then touched the tree on the west, north, east and south sides; he then lit his pipe and smoked it.

After the chiefs circled the tree in a victory dance, a 'man of impeccable character' was chosen to fell it, three other men being nominated as his assistants. The leader of the team stood at the west side, motioned with his axe three times towards the tree, then with his fourth swing struck it. The three assistants then followed in likewise manner. When the tree was nearly severed, the chiefs selected a person with 'a quiet and holy manner' to give the final blow. Great attention was paid to ensure that the falling tree did not touch the ground, and no one was allowed to step over it.

The cottonwood tree was chosen for its microcosmic nature; its leaves are patterned after the same geometry as the tipi, and the natural pattern of its trunk, seen in cross-section, is a five-pointed star, which to the Oglala Sioux represented the presence of the Great Spirit. After the felling ceremony, the tree was carried towards the place of its re-erection by six men, who set the tree upon poles and pointed its base eastwards towards the hole prepared for it. After various other rituals, the tree was raised and set in the hole, a little dance was held around the place, and the surrounding lodge was prepared by putting 28 forked sticks (a number perhaps representing the days of the lunar month) upright in a circle around the holy tree.

The Sun Dance lodge was then completed by the erection of a symbolic roof composed of 28 poles. The explicit intention was the creation of the universe in a likeness; each of the 28 posts around the perimeter represented some particular aspect of creation. The central omphalos pole of the sacred cottonwood tree itself represented *wakan-tanka*, the Great Spirit who is the centre of everything. The lodge's entrance was at the east, the direction from which the sun enters the world each day.

Such complex ritual and symbolism in the founding of a sacred edifice was typical rather than exceptional. The circular structure was seen as the microcosm, centred on a pole which was the outward manifestation of the omphalos. Round buildings have invariably centred upon some focal object of great importance. Most Christian buildings however have subsequently lost this central feature through the agency of iconoclasts, but one example is the central stone at St Michael's, Fulda, West Germany.

The universal nature of the circle was deemed apt for the shrine of all the gods of ancient Rome – the Pantheon, which was constructed as a vast semicircular dome. From the megalithic era onwards, round edifices have repeatedly been erected in Europe. Wooden structures like the so-called 'Woodhenge' and the Overton Hill 'Sanctuary' (which are known solely from post-hole remains) paralleled the structure and perhaps the function of the later North American Medicine lodges.

Stonehenge is another such structure. Circular temples were relatively common in ancient Greece, e.g. at Delphi, and the pattern was transmitted with much else to Rome and modified in the characteristic fashion of that empire. The Roman round temples at Tivoli and Spalato have survived into the modern era. The former was a basic rotunda surrounded externally by columns after the Greek manner, whilst the latter, which was part of the palace complex constructed by the fanatical pagan emperor Diocletian, was the forerunner of later structures. Paradoxically, this temple, whose geometry is based on the octagon, served as the model for Christian round churches. This similarity is not surprising when it is recalled that the underlying geometrical symbolism in Christian and pagan buildings is identical. Churches such as San Vitale at Ravenna were designed as microcosms of the world, and San

An eighteenth-century view of the interior of the Holy Sepulchre Church at Jerusalem, built on the legendary site of the tomb of Christ. As the central shrine of Christendom, and a focus for pilgrimage, the site was naturally associated with the compas – the Hebrew centre of the world.

Donato Bramante's circular Tempietto of St Peter Montorio, Rome, sanctifies the site of St Peter's inverted crucifixion.

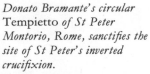

Vitale also possesses a pavement labyrinth, itself an image of the world. It served as a model for the later Christian churches such as the Chapel Palatine of the emperor Charlemagne at Aachen.

Round churches are perhaps best known as a result of their association with the Knights Templar, an occult chivalric order set up in the twelfth century with the ostensible purpose of protecting pilgrims on the roads to Jerusalem. However their activities began, the Knights Templar soon became very wealthy and powerful, and commenced the construction of round churches all over Europe and the Near East. The circular form of the churches was seen as a microcosm of the world, a reproduction of the original Church of the Holy Sepulchre in Jerusalem, which stood on the reputed site of the tomb of Christ. Stow, in his *Survey of London*, 1598, wrote:

Many noble men in all parts of Christendom became brethren of this order, and built themselves temples in every city or great town in England, but this at London was their chief house, which they built after the form of the temple near to the sepulchre of Our Lord at Jerusalem; they had also other temples in Cambridge, Bristow, Canterbury, Dover, Warwick. . . .

Of the many which once existed, there are now only five surviving churches of the Templar pattern in Britain. All these underwent extensive restoration during the nineteenth century. The survivors are at London, Cambridge, Little Maplestead, Northampton and Ludlow Castle. After the order was suppressed in 1314, the churches passed into other hands, and the practice of building circular churches lapsed.

However, at the Renaissance round churches again came into favour. The principles governing their geometry were rediscovered after centuries of disuse when the Renaissance architects began to study ancient texts and buildings. These new round churches, based on classical architectural models, were placed at the most significant geomantic points in the manner of the Holy Sepulchre itself. In Rome, Donato Bramante's *tempietto* of St Peter Montorio was such a church. Erected on the reputed site of St Peter's crucifixion, it celebrated symbolically 'the Rock' upon which the church arose.

In many cosmologies, the world was represented by a square. Like the circle, the square is a symbol with unique properties, but unlike the fluid and somewhat indefinite nature of the circle, the square is rigid and unyielding, symbolic of permanence and inflexibility. Just as the circle represents the heavenly plane of the spirits, so the square symbolizes the stable plane of matter. Where a building combines both elements, square and circle, there is embodied a reconciliation and fusion of the two planes to reconstitute the whole universe of spirit and matter.

A fundamental mystery in sacred geometry and alchemy was the squaring of the circle. By this is meant the production of a square with the same area as a circle, or the same circumference. It was implicit in the mysteries of alchemy. In the *Rosarium Philosophorum*, an ancient alchemical treatise, we find the following:

One of the five surviving round churches in England, the Holy Sepulchre in Cambridge. Although almost completely rebuilt in 1841, its original dimensions have been retained.

> *Make a round circle of the man and the woman,*
> *and draw out of this a square, and out of the*
> *square a triangle. Make a round circle and you*
> *will have the stone of the philosophers.*

The image of the circle squared represents in psychological terms the archetype of wholeness. The triangle and square are natural products of the construction of the vesica. The achievement of the reconciliation of the incommensurable is the starting-point for temple construction, and buildings whose geometry contains both square and circle occur in every continent. The goal of geomancer and alchemist is ultimately the same: the reconciliation of disparate elements leading to the knowledge of God.

The square

Not all buildings which incorporate the square into their ground plans, façades or elevations use the circle. The square is mystically linked with the solidity of the

The Taj Mahal at Agra, India, incorporates traditional Islamic sacred geometry, the ground plans of both the mausoleum and the grounds being determined by ad quadratum.

earth, and, almost invariably, square buildings erected to geomantic principles are orientated 'foursquare'; each side faces a cardinal point which, if determined by astronomical observation, will be very near to true; if by compass, it will show secular variation. The Egyptian pyramids are the most spectacular monuments possessing square ground plans. They were orientated towards true north-south with astonishing precision, and were constructed to rigorous standards of accuracy. The noted Egyptologist, Sir Flinders Petrie, surveyed the Great Pyramid and was impressed by the phenomenal accuracy of its orientation, which deviates by less than five minutes of arc from true north-south. Petrie, and others after him, believed that the axis of the earth had shifted rather than the pyramid being even this inaccurate, a theory backed up by recent research into plate tectonics and continental drift.

Although the square is a relatively simple figure to lay out, it still has remarkable geometrical properties. It is capable of precise division by two and multiples of two, without any need for measurement. The holy or cosmic city layout is thus derived simply by bisecting the sides, drawing a cross which divides the area into four. At the centre of this cross is the omphalos. The square and its multiples form the ground plans of many of the world's greatest monuments: the pyramids in Egypt and Mexico, Babylonian ziggurats, the Holy Oblation of the Jews, Santa Sophia at Constantinople, the Taj Mahal. Related to the square as microcosm of

the earth are the four directions, which, as we have
seen, are associated in many cultures with guardian
beasts or gods, as well as special colours and attributes.

The double square was the form of the enclosure of
the tabernacle of the Jews, which itself was a triple
square. The Holy of Holies occupied a single square.
The double square was later used as the basis of the
ground plan of many Armenian churches, and also of St
Paul's Cathedral in London. From the square is derived
the system known to the medieval masons as *ad
quadratum*, one square superimposed upon another
whose orientation differs by 45°, thus producing the
'octagram'. This is again easy to lay out with string and
compasses, the method adopted by all ancient surveyors.

Ad quadratum underlies very many ancient structures. Representing the intermediate stage between the
square of earth and the circle of heaven, the eightfold
symbolism fits in especially well with the eightfold path
of Buddhism, and the octad or octagram is also an
Islamic symbol especially sacred to the Sufis. The
ground plans of Chinese Confucian temples utilized the
octagram. But it was in the Romanesque and Gothic
periods of medieval European church architecture that
the system was developed to its most complex and
refined form. The original geometry of the building
was often expanded when new extensions and recon-
structions were carried out. A perfect example of this
exists at Ely Cathedral, where all extensions were made

*Largest of square-based
buildings, the pyramids of the
Gizeh group, the tombs of the
kings Khufu, Khafre and
Menkaure.*

The *mausoleum of Ilkhan Uljaitu at Sultaneih, Persia (*c. *1307), embodies constructional principles used a few years later at Ely Cathedral, England – sacred geometry which transcended religions.*

according to the original geometrical scheme. When Ely's central tower collapsed in 1322, the crossing was expanded from a square to an octagram, still exactly determined by the geometry. Interestingly, although the technical method of construction was Islamic (imported during the Crusades), based upon the mausoleum of Ilkhan Uljaitu at Sultaneih in Persia (1307–13), the geometry was the guiding principle. At Ely, the octagon reigns supreme. Above the omphalos is a carving of Christ in majesty, giving the benediction in the middle of a beautifully complex web of lierne vaulting ribs which are themselves related to the points of the compass by the orientation of the whole cathedral. From this centre, the geometry expands, encompassing the whole building, its subdivision marking such vital points as the position of pillars and the springing of the vaulting. Ely's geometry also involves *ad triangulum* as a subsystem (see below), a geometrical combination shared with Glastonbury Abbey, once the most sacred shrine of England. In different forms, the schemata extant at Ely can be found all over Europe.

The geometrical systems underlying late Christian architecture are not the subject of speculation, but part of a well attested and continuous tradition. Several sets of working drawings still exist, showing the principles of geometry involved in the layout of churches in the medieval period. One well-known source of information is the so-called sketchbook of Villard de Honnecourt, an itinerant mason who noted down various systems of design, and also individual examples. Less well-known are the surviving scale drawings of several German master masons. Among these are the original elevation for the west front of Strasbourg Cathedral, drawn in about 1385 by Michael Parler. There are also the designs for the steeple of Ulm Minster, made by Matthäus Böblinger between 1474 and 1492. When the plan was rediscovered in the last century, the spire was completed from it. The continued existence of the working drawings of Strasbourg Cathedral is probably owing to the extremely late survival there of a lodge of operative masons. It was finally wound up in 1777.

Ad quadratum was one of the most persistent systems of sacred geometry. Employed throughout the Romanesque and Gothic periods of church construction, it survived to become the dominant system in the Renaissance. The cathedral of Florence, which spans the period between the Gothic and the Renaissance,

Working drawing, c. 1385, by the master mason Michael Parler for the west front of Strasbourg Cathedral.

was constructed on a plan of a series of octagons. One was the basis for the dome, which symbolizes the fusion of the earth and the heavens.

The events which formed the background to the construction of Milan Cathedral encapsulate the principles and application of sacred geometry as they had become formalized by the end of the fourteenth century.

No fewer than 50 names are mentioned in the archives in connection with the design and foundation stages during the cathedral's first fifteen years. Despite this plethora of experts, a severe geometrical problem soon engulfed the project – a quarrel between the proponents of *ad quadratum* and *ad triangulum*, a section based upon the equilateral triangle. Severe mathematical problems now presented themselves, for, while the height of a square is obviously related to a similar square on the ground plan, the height of an equilateral triangle is incommensurable with its side.

The Italian masons soldiered on until more problems forced them to appoint French consultants under the master mason Jean Mignot. But in 1400, Mignot had a bitter argument with the Italian masons. The following year he departed for Paris, and left the Italians to continue unaided. The cathedral's construction went on for many years until finally completed on the orders of Napoleon in 1809.

Milan is also interesting as the only Gothic cathedral whose inherent geometry has been used to illustrate the tenets of the Roman architectural theorist Vitruvius. In Cesare Cesariano's 1521 edition of Vitruvius's *Ten Books of Architecture*, the plan and elevation of Milan Cathedral are shown with superimposed lines demonstrating the geometrical principles upon which the cathedral was finally erected – *ad quadratum* for the ground plan, and *ad triangulum* for the elevation.

This elevation in Cesariano's edition is of note as the origin of the cross-section and elevation of the Expiatory Temple of the Sagrada Familia, the *magnum opus* of the Catalan mystical architect Antoni Gaudí. Cesariano's work recorded the 'rules of the German architects' as follows: 1. A method of fixing the overall length and breadth of the church by means of the vesica piscis. 2. The subdivision of this plan into equal bays. 3. The determination of the heights of various parts by means of equilateral triangles based upon the lengths of these subdivisions. Attempts to fuse these rules with *ad quadratum* were bound to cause problems.

The arguments and uncertainty which beset the designers and executors of Milan Cathedral serve to remind us that there was never one rigid system of sacred geometry which was applied like a rule of iron in all circumstances. On the contrary, disagreements and alterations were as common then as now. One fundamental difference, however, is that in the past the disagreements were between different schools of opinion, all of whom nevertheless were operating within a framework of canonical geometry.

The triangle

The triangle by itself is a rich source of arcane symbolism. In Christian iconography, it represents the

Holy Trinity of God the Father, God the Son and God the Holy Ghost. Symbol of godhead in several other cosmologies, the equilateral triangle drawn with its apex uppermost symbolizes the celestial, active or male principle. In alchemical iconography, it stands for that most active of states, fire. Conversely, the triangle with its apex at the lowest point represents the passive or female attribute, the alchemical symbol for water.

When the two triangles are combined, forming the hexagram or Star of David, the disparate elements of the universe can be said to be reintegrated into the primordial whole.

The geometry which generates this figure is directly related to the vesica piscis. If a vesica piscis is laterally bisected, and the ends of the line are connected to the two apices of the vesica, then two equilateral triangles are formed base to base.

The triangle has rarely been used in isolation for the construction of buildings, as three-sided structures are decidedly impractical. However, the geometrical system of *ad triangulum* has been found to underlie many ancient buildings, including Greek and Roman temples such as the Temple of Zeus at Olympia and the Pantheon in Rome. Unlike *ad quadratum*, it fell from favour and was rarely applied in the early and mid-medieval period. But it appeared with a vengeance in the fifteenth century, and even forced out *ad quadratum* in some places.

In England, the best example of the use of *ad triangulum* was at King's College Chapel in Cambridge. The chapel's plan is based upon the use of the equilateral triangle, from which is derived the positions of all the major features of the ground plan, the walls and vaulting, the dimensions of the side chantries and the positions of the four end towers. The chapel was constructed with the use of sacred geometry combined with mystically determined dimensions, as were many cathedrals in Europe.

A late manifestation of the medieval Catholic spirit in England was the Triangular Lodge at Rushton in Northamptonshire. A purely triangular building dedicated to the Christian Trinity, it was erected after the Reformation by Sir Thomas Tresham at his country estate. One of the few completely triangular buildings in the world, it was constructed in 1595 as a devotional exercise. Every part of the lodge is emblematic of the Holy Trinity.

Surprisingly, the lodge still stands today, having survived periods when Puritan fanatics would have had

The triangle: Sir Thomas Tresham's unique embodiment of the Mysteries of the Holy Trinity – the Triangular Lodge at Rushton, Northants.

the power and the inclination to single out such a target for their zealous hooliganism. But the Triangular Lodge went unharmed. It remains mute testimony to a lost way of thought.

The cross

The cross is best known as a Christian symbol, but of course it predates that religion by many centuries, being one of the most ancient hieroglyphs to occur in rock-scribings. Nor has its use in architecture been restricted to churches. The cross is the form of the roads to the four cardinal points, centred at the omphalos, and is derived from the quartering of the circle, Jung's archetype of wholeness.

The equal-armed cross, which in architectural terms is produced from five contiguous squares (one at the centre and four for the directions), is often called the Greek cross. Despite its name, buildings of this shape are not restricted to Greece; sacred architecture from ancient Mexico to Ethiopia has used the form, and earthworks in this form have been found in places as far apart as England and North America.

But the cross is nevertheless *par excellence* the emblem of Christianity, the instrument of execution upon which, Christians believe, Christ was tortured to death. Honorius of Autun wrote in *De gemma animale* (*c.* 1330):

Churches made in the form of a cross show how people of the church are crucified by this world; those made round in the form of a circle show that the church is built throughout the circuit of the globe to become the circle of the crown of eternity through love.

Honorius's reference to the cruciform church as emblematic of the Crucifixion repeats an ancient belief that the temple was literally the body of God. The building was not only the residence of the deity, as in the Holy of Holies in Solomon's Temple, but its actual fabric was in some mysterious way transmuted into God's body in the same manner as the bread and wine of the Eucharist. Several medieval and Renaissance illustrations exist which show this mystic transformation, the figure of Christ upon the ground plan of the church. Man the microcosm was scaled up: his body, the original perfect temple, was symbolically reproduced in a temple made by the hands of men (p. 171).

The pentagram

The pentagram, a figure of great importance in ritual magic, is often shown with a superimposed body of a man for, like the cross, it represents the macrocosm, and through this correspondence it was possible to work sympathetic magic. In its upright form it was suitable for the practice of white magic; inverted it became the emblem of evil at work. According to Professor Rudolf Koch in his *The Book of Signs* (1930), the pentagram signified a witch's foot to the Celtic priests, to the Jews it represented the five Mosaic books, and to the Druids it stood for the symbol of godhead. In Christian symbolism, it represents the mystery of the rosary, and by analogy with the rose, the Virgin Mary.

The pentagram is fundamental to the geometry of harmonious proportion, since it is the figure from which the Golden Section is derived. This is the ratio between the side of the pentagon drawn between the points of a pentagram, and the side of the pentagram itself. The actual figure is 1:1.618014, a ratio which produces shapes both aesthetically pleasing and of mystical importance, and which is found to underlie the proportions of many ancient Greek and Roman temples. Renaissance painters like Leonardo and Raphael constantly used this geometry as a basis for their work, and it has been continued in unbroken tradition through to the present day.

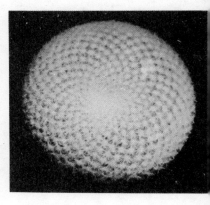

The natural organic spirals of a cactus grow according to the mathematical formula of the Fibonacci Series, which is directly related to the Golden Section, demonstrating the underlying geometry of creation.

Directly related to the Golden Section is the Fibonacci Series, a mathematical concept which was first observed by Leonardo Fibonacci (Leonardo da Pisa) in the thirteenth century. Since his time, biologists have established that it is also a basic principle in nature. The Fibonacci Series is found in numerous natural formations: the leaves on trees, the skins of onions, the arrangement of pads on cats' feet, the shells of microscopic protozoa, and many organically produced spiral structures. Its production is deceptively simple. The last two numbers in a sequence are added together to give the next number, and so on, i.e. 1, 1, 2, 3, 5, 8, 13, 21, 34, 55 etc. It is directly related in geometry to the Golden Section by way of the equiangular spiral, a geometrical form which determines, among other things, the shape of rams' horns and of nautilus shells. Each section of the spiral relates to the next section in the sequence in the same progression as the Fibonacci Series. As the numbers rise, their ratios correspondingly creep closer and closer to the Golden Section.

In recent architecture, this proportional system was applied by Le Corbusier in his *modulor*, a method of determining harmonious proportion based upon the Golden Section and the Fibonacci Series. In his book

The tomb of the Gothic king Theodoric at Ravenna, Italy, is based upon the decagon – the fusion of the upright and the inverted pentagram.

Modulor (1951), Le Corbusier discussed the ancient proportional systems of Egypt, Greece and medieval Europe, where he showed the use of the Golden Section. These uses were, of course, in hidden geometry – the basis for the building, not the exoteric form. The pentagon and its double, the decagon, are rarely found as such, though the tomb of Theodoric, king of the Goths, at Ravenna in Italy, is decagonal, symbolic of the fusion of opposites to recreate the whole.

To lay out a pentagram or pentagon is a much more complicated task than to lay out a circle, triangle or square. So although fivefold symmetry occurs regularly in the details of Gothic tracery and carving, it is exceptional in the overall form both of churches and of secular buildings. One of the few pentagonal sacred buildings to be put up was designed by Giovanni Santini (1667–1723), member of a family of Italian Freemasons, who constructed churches in a peculiar Gothic-Baroque synthesis which in some ways foreshadowed *Art nouveau*. The town of Žd'ár in Moravia contains his strangest creation, the 'Pilgrim Church on the Green Hill', which not only possesses a pentagonal ground plan, but also five oval side chapels. However, the best-known, if not the most loved, of pentagonal buildings is of course the Pentagon in Washington, though this is profane architecture with no arcane relationship with the cosmos.

Magic squares

Sacred architecture has always been based upon sacred geometry, with the additional use of numerical 'tricks' like the Fibonacci Series and magic squares, i.e. squares of numbers whose sequences add up to the same figure, whether the adding be done vertically, horizontally, or diagonally. Magic squares are now considered little more than mathematical oddities which produce pleasing patterns when drawn out. They are found in books intended for the young, an example of the way that the mystical side of consciousness has been largely driven out of the adult world, and relegated to the realms of mythology and fairy tale.

Traditionally magic squares embody in their numerology the attributes of a particular astrological planet. Seven such astrologically linked squares exist, dedicated to Saturn, Jupiter, Mars, the Sun, Venus, Mercury and the Moon, that of Saturn being the smallest and that of the moon the largest. From their sequences are generated sigils (symbols of the planet) whose patterns, occultists claim, have controlled the forms and attributes of the Seven Wonders of the World. The Temple of Solomon was said to be astrologically ruled by the square of Saturn, and the Temple of Zeus at Olympia by Jupiter. The Hanging Gardens of Babylon belonged to the square of Mars, the Colossus of Rhodes was controlled by the square of the Sun, and the Mausoleum at Halicarnassus by Venus. Mercury's magic square was the controlling sigil of the Pyramids of Egypt, and the Moon ruled the Temple of Diana at Ephesus. How much these ruling attributes were geometrical, and how much they were esoteric remains an enigma. This system substitutes Solomon's Temple for the Pharos of Alexandria in the usual list of the Seven Wonders, as the latter was not a sacred building. John Michell has shown that the elevation of Lichfield Cathedral was based upon the hidden ratios of the upper portion of the magic square of Mars, the dedicated ruler of this former omphalos of England, and there are most likely many other sacred buildings of Europe and the Near East whose construction involved the use of this strange method of planning which determined, by esoteric geometry derived from the mathematics of the squares, the proportions and forms of the buildings.

A baroque interpretation of fivefold radial symmetry: ground plan of Santini's chapel of Svatý Jan Nepomucký at Žďár in Moravia, Czechoslovakia.

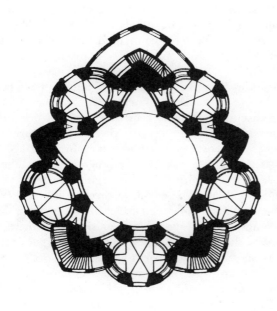

9

Measure

The hidden ratios of geometry make use of the inherent properties of Euclidean geometrical figures. But the hidden ratios of magic squares are dependent upon number. Number is the underlying factor which relates sacred architecture to its place in the cosmic order as perceived by its authors, expressed in terms of measure – metrology. Strictly, the term metrology is the study of measures. However, its meaning has become expanded to encompass the study and use of symbolic measures and dimensions in all aspects of geomancy, especially in relation to the incorporation of such dimensions in sacred buildings.

The dimensions of a building, mystically conceived as the microcosm, were formerly not dependent upon the constraints of finance or materials 'in stock', but upon the prevailing cosmological beliefs and religious concepts. Various people from time to time have put forward extravagant claims concerning the Great Pyramid on this basis, which, strangely, cannot be applied to the scores of other existing pyramids. Better preserved and better documented buildings may hold the key to our understanding of symbolic measure in sacred places.

Angkor Wat, the Cambodian temple of Vishnu, whose astronomical alignments and orientations have been discussed elsewhere in this book, is one of the most striking examples of such architecture constructed to incorporate symbolic measure. Angkor Wat was laid out in the ancient Khmer measure, the *hat* (17.12 in.). The dimensions of significant parts of the temple are related to periods of the astronomical cycles of the world and the sacred cycles of Hindu cosmology. In common with special sacred sites elsewhere, the temple's dimensions were laid out with painstaking precision, with an error of less than 0.1%. Such universally precise measures were rendered necessary by geomantic considerations – the accuracy of markers for the observation of astronomical phenomena, the precise orientation, and the sacred dimensions.

Angkor Wat integrates all these considerations. Positioned on a sunrise alignment to the hill of Phnom

Bok, 10.88 miles away, and a winter solstice alignment with the temple of Prasat Kuk Bangro, 3.43 miles to the southeast, the internal measurements of Angkor Wat are partially determined by solar orientations. The dimensions of the building, which embody its sacred purpose, are thus cunningly combined with its function as an observatory. The central temple is approached by a long causeway, a literal and metaphorical journey from an open expanse of horizontal space in bright daylight which gradually changes to the enclosed, vertical darkness of the central tower above the omphalos, a gradual shifting of the psychological awareness of the pilgrim to prepare him for the powers resident there. The dimensions of the causeway are so contrived that the visitor reenacts the phases of Hindu sacred history in the course of the transit along the approach path.

All important parts of the temple are related to cosmological intervals. In Hindu sacred history there are four time periods or Yugas which together compose one cycle. They begin with a Golden Age, the Krita Yuga, and progress through Treta Yuga, Dvapara Yuga to the Kali Yuga. The last two periods are the worst, and the geomancers at Angkor have appropriately placed them at the furthest distance from the sanctuary. Thus the vast rectangular moat which surrounds the whole temple has a width of 439 *hat*, symbolizing the 432,000-year cycle of the Kali Yuga, the last and most decadent age of man. Incidentally, discrepancies between the temple's dimensions and the era lengths can be accounted for by the need to achieve the best fit between symbolic lengths and the astronomical alignments, which are of course fixed. From the first step of the western entrance gateway to the balustrade wall at the end of the causeway is 867 *hat*, symbolizing the 864,000-year period of the Dvapara Yuga. Thence to the central tower is 1,296 *hat*, corresponding to the 1,296,000 years of the Treta Yuga; and the distance between the first step of the bridge to the geomantic centre of the temple is 1,734 *hat*, which represents the 1,728,000-year period of the Krita Yuga.

Other dimensions of Angkor Wat correspond with the number of months in a year and the cycles of the Hindu lunar calendar. The interior axial lengths of the nine chambers in the inner tower represent the number of constellations of the Hindu zodiac along the ecliptic. The exterior axial length of the topmost elevation, like the height of St Paul's Cathedral in London, stands for the number of days in a year with a length of 365.37 *hat*, whilst the distance between the floor of the north and south libraries in the second gallery and the sacred relics of the temple correspond in *hat* with the length of a lunar month, 29.53 days. Numerous other astronomical dimensions are interwoven with the dimensions of the structure. Angkor Wat is thus a typical example of the temple as embodiment of the religious faith, equivalent to the Gothic cathedrals of Europe as a *summa theologia* – a representation in stone of all the aspects of the universal order reflected in the religious life and creed. All over the world we find such symbolism, the dimensions of the building directly reflecting the arcane secrets of whichever mystery the temple represents.

In many legendary histories, sacred measures were sacred precisely because they were given by the gods to the human race in general, and to the temple builders in particular. King Henry VI of England saw himself in this light when he founded King's College in Cambridge, for he gave precise metrological directions on how it was to be built, taking special care to stipulate the exact dimensions of the chapel and other buildings. Owing to the vagaries of finance and a civil war, only the chapel was ever built according to the King's instructions, but this at least was executed exactly as he had ordered. As one of the last Gothic churches to be constructed by masons in the old tradition and according to the old principles, it embodied in its fabric, dimensions, proportions, colours and geometry the basic mysteries of the faith.

The ground plan of King's College Chapel is very simple, as there is not one free-standing pillar anywhere. It is a massive building, longer than the cathedral at Oxford, and far larger than the needs of a relatively small college. To erect the chapel, the main street of Cambridge had to be closed, and many houses, shops and inns were demolished, causing a number of riots. From the foundation in 1446, work went on sporadically until the stonework was finally completed in 1515. Despite dynastic changes in the monarchy (who largely paid for the chapel), and a crippling civil war, the chapel's construction continued as if it were indeed a sacred duty. The special nature of the dimensions and numerology reinforces this view.

The chapel's proportions are based upon a ground plan produced by twelve Pythagorean triangles of 5:12:13 four-foot modules. Numerologically, the number 26 is dominant. There are 26 great stained-glass windows, 26 structural uprights, 26 ribs in each pair of

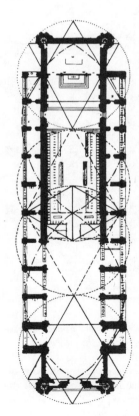

Left, the arrangement of John Wastell's sixteenth-century fan vaulting at King's College Chapel, Cambridge, is directly determined by the ad triangulum *geometry of Reginald Ely's ground plan (below), laid out 69 years earlier.*

fans in the stone vaulting, 26 apertures in each panel of side-chantry tracery, etc. The number 26 is a key symbol in kabbalistic *gematria*, a widely-used symbolic system in which the letters in Hebrew or Greek were given number equivalents. In this way, a name can be symbolized by a length in any predetermined unit. Twenty-six represents the ineffable name of God, in Hebrew יהוה. This word, the letters JHVH, permeates the fabric of the chapel as the spirit of God was believed to permeate the earth, making the chapel indeed the divine body. In fact, the numerological symbolism is openly revealed at the tympanum over the west door, where a seventeenth-century woodcarver has made manifest the mystery: in the centre of the tympanum, flanked by two palm trees and cherubs' heads, is the disc of the sun, in the centre of which is carved the Tetragrammaton, the Hebrew יהוה. Although its significance is lost on today's tourist guides (and most of today's tourists), it is perhaps the only overt statement of mystical purpose to exist on the outside of an English ecclesiastical building.

Number, name and measure are intricately inter-related in sacred buildings like King's College Chapel. To the initiate, merely to enter such a building was to see revealed the mysteries of the faith, recorded in a form hidden from the minds of the uninstructed. Services conducted within, where the architecture, orientation, music, incense, chants and vestments were all derived from the same canonical system of mystical mathematics, expressed in an immediate form the attempted reintegration of man with the cosmos.

The length of King's College Chapel is 288 feet, or 192 cubits. 192 is the gematrial number of the Greek MAPIAM, the name of the Virgin Mary, who is the principal patron of the college and its chapel. The length is also equal to the sum of the two kabbalistic sephiroth, Hesed (72) and Gevurah (216), which represent respectively Mercy and Power. Hesed is masculine and Gevurah is feminine, reflecting the synthesis inherent in the geometry of *ad triangulum* upon which the chapel is based, and also the dual male/female dedication to Our Lady and St Nicholas. As at Angkor Wat, many other dimensions are chosen especially for their symbolic properties.

In addition to these internal subtleties, it is evident that the chapel was deliberately located in a particular place, related like Glastonbury and Stonehenge to a nationwide geometry whose properties are yet to be elucidated in symbolic terms.

Post-Reformation sacred geometry in Europe

Although it differs little from the geometry practised by the medieval Freemasons, post-Reformation sacred geometry differs considerably in its manner of application. Until the Renaissance, the secrets of sacred geometry were more or less kept from interested but non-operative outsiders. As the ideas of the Renaissance filtered through from Italy into other parts of Europe, the masonic secrets were gradually published through the recently invented printing presses. In Germany Matthäus Röritzer, and in Spain Rodrigo Gil de Hontañon, published detailed but unauthorized expositions of sacred geometry as applied to churches. Hontañon actually used the work of Simon García, a mason who had lived 150 years earlier.

The Reformation led to a withdrawal of church patronage, and as the cultural climate changed the ancient secrets of the masons gradually ceased to be applied to church architecture. An intellectual interpretation of the works of Vitruvius, combined with a certain amount of divulged masonic lore, became dominant, and the mason's supreme position was pushed aside by a new breed – the architects. The ancient techniques of Gothic architecture, handed down and refined over the centuries, were suppressed by the new intelligentsia whose rejection of the

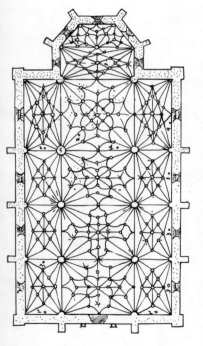

As their power waned, medieval masonic traditions were made public: Rodrigo Gil de Hontañon's Compendium of Architecture *(1681) published the works of Simon García, such as this design for a vaulted church.*

medieval spirit also included a rejection of medieval religion. A revived, if altered, classical Roman architecture took over, designed by the architect not as the Great Work or the *Summa Theologia*, but as an intellectual or aesthetic exercise based upon personal interpretation rather than upon a religious canon.

Vitruvius's *Ten Books of Architecture*, which had been largely forgotten for a millennium, were taken as a starting-point for the architecture of the new era. The Italian styles of Palladio and Alberti were consciously based upon this Roman theoretician, as we can see from the proliferation of tributes to his principles amongst the writings of the architects who moulded the new aesthetics. However, although the Gothic sacred geometry was cut off, the principle which ruled earlier temples now came again to the fore – the Golden Section. The central idea of Renaissance philosophy, the Golden Section or Divine Proportion, was both magical and geometrical in its inspiration. Luca Pacioli's seminal work, *De Divina Proportione*, was a major influence on contemporary and later architects, restating in the terms of the Renaissance the ancient and eternal relation of number, ratio and geometry in the reflection of cosmic and human proportions.

Geomancy at this period was beginning to disintegrate before the new ideas which were challenging the hegemony of the Church and its clients. A more inward-looking approach took the place of the systems of interrelating sites which had been the guiding principle in England as late as the mid-fifteenth century. Purely visual in approach, and based upon the recent discovery of perspective by Italian artists, the architects now created parkland and vistas, 'settings' for architecture analogous to the setting of jewels. The mysteries retreated into the books of magicians like Dr John Dee who, though immersed in Pythagorean, Platonic, and Vitruvian theories, failed to make much impression upon the practising architects of the time.

In Spain, where the tradition of mystical, geomantically determined architecture has continued into the modern era, these mystical mathematics, based on classical ideas, were reflected in the work of another great Renaissance architect, Juan Herrera, royal architect to King Philip II, who helped design the Escorial. Both Herrera and Philip were deeply involved in magic and astrology, being ardent followers of the mathematical mystic Ramón Lull, and were also collectors of the works of Hermes Trismegistus and his disciples. The proportion and design of the Escorial are

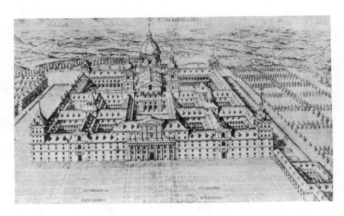

based upon the Jesuit Villalpanda's occult works on the
Vision of Ezekiel (1596) and his reconstruction of the
destroyed temple at Jerusalem.

Despite the great interest in Vitruvius, consciously
Vitruvian architecture was not built in England until
the early seventeenth century. In the 1620s, Inigo
Jones, known as 'Vitruvius Britannicus', the architect
to the court of King Charles I, desgined various
buildings, including the Covent Garden church,
according to Vitruvian ideas. In addition to his
pioneering of work as an architect, Jones was also the
first person to try to evaluate the underlying geometry
of Stonehenge, which in his opinion was a Vitruvian
design of Roman origin. His findings and theories were
posthumously published in *The Most Notable Antiquity
of Great Britain vulgarly called Stone-Heng on Salisbury
Plain, restored by Inigo Jones, Architect to the late King*
(1655). When this book was reprinted in 1725, it
influenced the architect and planner John Wood Jr,
whose construction of the Bath Circus was based
directly upon Jones's plans and proportions of
Stonehenge! Jones's grand designs, which included the
reconstruction of St Paul's Cathedral, were never
realized owing to the revolution which overthrew both
king and court and even attempted to suppress sacred
architecture. As architect of St Paul's, Jones built a new
Vitruvian façade at the west end in 1633, but no more
was done.

In 1666, when the cathedral was finally burnt, along
with much of London, the opportunity to rebuild was
presented to Sir Christopher Wren. Although it was the
only true Protestant cathedral of the seventeenth
century, and largely Renaissance in detail, St Paul's was
built largely according to the old Gothic principles of
construction. Based upon Ely Cathedral, where Sir
Christopher's uncle, Matthew Wren, had been bishop

from 1638 to 1667 (including seventeen years in prison during the Commonwealth), the engineering for the dome was modelled on Ely's octagon and lantern, the only Gothic dome in the country.

St Paul's was originally designed as an octagonal church with a slightly longer nave, and as in Wren's design, it was based on *ad quadratum*. The final design, approved by the alchemist king Charles II, was a perfect blend of Gothic and Vitruvian principles, but in its geometry, based upon a double square, St Paul's reflects the ancient cathedral scheme. Wren himself was after all the master of an operative lodge of Freemasons who, under Mr Strong, were employed on the construction of the last of the old cathedrals erected in England. Perhaps the greatest of English architects, the designer of St Paul's Cathedral had sufficient intuitive ability to merge the traditional and the older, but revived, systems in a new synthesis.

Several continental Baroque architects utilized a similar Gothic-Vitruvian synthesis to determine the ground plans and façades of their churches. Most notable of these was Balthasar Neumann (born 1687), who was remarkable for having started his career as a military engineer – an ironic inversion of the careers of English master masons of the mid-sixteenth century. His use of the old Gothic proportional systems is especially noticeable in the pilgrim church of *Vierzehn-heiligen* in West Germany, proving that even then the tradition was not dead, but merely modified to suit new ideas.

An interesting revival of the masonic connection with cathedral building took place as late as 1882, when the unsafe central tower of Peterborough Cathedral was pulled down and reconstructed. A plaque records that the hierarchy of the Freemasons under Lord Caernarvon reconsecrated it 'with full masonic form'.

The brilliant Catalan architect and mystic Antoni Gaudí (1852–1926) is a figure of controversy even to this day. Few of his works survive, and many of these are unfinished or mutilated. His architecture is often classified as *Art nouveau*, but in reality it is a complete departure from anything previously built. Many of his works were constructed in the tradition of the medieval freemasons as acts of worship. Gaudí was fanatically devout, with a special piety towards the Virgin Mary, and in later years he would walk miles to and from his place of work each day to hear Mass.

In Catalonia, which has a strong nationalistic and anarchist background, there has long been a mystical

tradition of architecture, derived both from Spanish and Arabic tendencies in sacred buildings. Gaudí's position as inheritor of an ancient geomantic tradition is well illustrated in the Park Güell, built in Barcelona between 1900 and 1914. The park, which is still a favourite resort of Barcelonans, occupies a district in the Muntamana Pelada near the slopes of Tibidabo. Gaudí synthesized a new world from architecture and nature, a geomantic transformation of what might have been merely a garden city like Letchworth into an expression of western Christian Feng-Shui. It has been argued by art historians with no knowledge of geomancy that the Park Güell should be interpreted as the most fully developed expression of landscape architecture in the traditions of the sixteenth and seventeenth century. However, in his masterful integration of the natural and artificial, Gaudí went much further, creating it in the spirit of ancient geomantic works. Its patterns may seem capricious, but they have been verified by dowsers to be the patterns inherent in the earth at that place.

The Park Güell is a relatively little-known masterpiece. The Sagrada Familia temple, although only a fragment of the complete building, is known throughout the world – there is simply nothing like it. This temple was the *chef d'oeuvre* in which Gaudí saw the fulfilment of his destiny as architect, geomancer and performer of the Great Work. He believed his mission to be the glorification of God by creating the perfect microcosm, and he set out to do it.

The Sagrada Familia temple was begun in 1882, not by Gaudí, but Francisco de Paula del Villar, who had been commissioned by the publisher José Matia Bocabella to build a church dedicated to St Joseph, his namesake, and the Holy Family. It was intended to be a symbol of the rebirth of the city of Barcelona. Villar's building was neo-Gothic in concept and plan, but a dispute arose between him and Juan Martorell,

Rudolf Steiner's first Goetheanum, an organic building made of an organic material – wood – and destroyed by fire in 1922.

Bocabella's advisor, and the project was abandoned after only part of the crypt had been completed. Martorell called in Gaudí, who transformed the building into the geomantic masterpiece we can see from his surviving drawings and the small part which was actually completed.

Like the ancient temples and cathedrals, the Sagrada Familia was conceived as a microcosm of Creation, according to a detailed and coherent system of symbolism. Its cross-section, though stripped of the constructional necessities of the Gothic masters, was based upon the masonic system *ad triangulum* derived from Cesariano's drawings of Milan Cathedral, a continuity of mystic principles across the centuries. Today, it remains unfinished. Gaudí's plans and models were partly destroyed by anticlerical anarchists during the Spanish Revolution, though they were subsequently reconstructed by his followers.

Although he did not work on principles governed by ancient traditions, Rudolf Steiner's architectural works were also designed according to principles which come under the aegis of geomantic buildings. Founder of the Anthroposophical movement, in 1913 Steiner designed the *Goetheanum* at Dornach in Switzerland as the headquarters of his organization. The original Goetheanum, which was made mainly of wood, was destroyed by arsonists, but it was replaced by another building on the same site. In its layout, design and forms, it embodied the theoretical premises of Anthroposophy and the concepts of evolution of art in an organic sequence, derived from Goethe's theory of metamorphosis. The art of eurhythmy, the controlled interpretation of the sound-quality of music and speech in movement, was perfected in the Goetheanum, an event Steiner believed would never have occurred without the building – a truly geomantic attitude.

Although Steiner stated categorically that the Goetheana were not temples, but 'Houses of Speech',

The Mormon Temple in Salt Lake Valley, Utah. Two days after the Mormons' arrival, Brigham Young made a mark on the ground and proclaimed, 'Here we will build a temple to our God.' The building was completed 40 years later.

their unified embodiment of scientific, artistic, religious, architectural and symbolic aspects closely followed the ancient synthesis of traditional temples. Apart from the Goetheana, a number of other buildings have been erected after the principles of Anthroposophy. Their origins are made plain by the lecture Steiner gave to farmers in 1924, when he expounded the age-old concept of two main forces, the cosmic and the earthly, which must be in balance in order that healthy soil may result – the selfsame principles encountered in the founding of the omphalos in ancient times. Architects look upon Steiner, like Gaudí, as an eccentric wanderer from the mainstream of world architecture, which is now based solely upon cost effectiveness.

Even today Mormon temples, which are erected with remarkable regularity in various parts of the world, embody sacred dimensions, based in the main on Biblical models. The mother temple in Salt Lake City, Utah, whose site was divined by the Mormon prophet Brigham Young, is the prototype for all the others. The symbolic 40 years were taken to construct the temple, which, in the tradition, contains various rooms painted to represent different eras of the Biblical period, and baptismal fonts which, standing on the back of twelve bronze oxen, three for each of the four directions, exactly reproduce the 'molten sea' or container of sacred water in Solomon's celebrated temple.

Despite these isolated examples, the few sacred buildings which are erected in this secular age have little in common with the temples of old. Mystical geometry is unknown to their architects, who build upon sites which tend to be chosen simply because they are available. The study of such matters is now relegated to the lodges of speculative Freemasons and institutes of geomantic research.

The urbanization of the countryside

10

Urbanization of the countryside is the inevitable result of urban control and regulation. From its original natural state to its present condition, this urbanization of the countryside has been a long and uneven progression, but the ultimate result is the remodelling of a natural landscape into the image of the city. It has taken place concurrently with the centralization of control, and the transition from federal or tribal forms of organization to nationhood. It has involved the imposition of a new order upon the old which, since it is fundamentally derived from the natural features and cycles of the earth, does not fit in with the exercise of centralized order. Government, requiring funds, imposed taxation upon production. In order to enable the authorities to regulate this taxation, standardized systems of land measure were brought to bear on the natural random variation. In the ancient world, this reordering was originally performed by theocratic government, which still related the division to the local geomancy.

The earliest recorded land division systems were in Sumeria and Egypt, where taxation was the spur to their implementation. The Romans reordered the ancient land divisions by a method known as centuriation – the dividing of land areas into a geometrical grid of squares. The Roman system of augury, a technique to find the correct place on the countryside from which the survey could originate, always preceded the technical laying-out of an area. Inherited from the Romans' predecessors, the Etruscans, the augurs' rituals are described in the works of the Roman governor of Britain and aqueduct designer Frontinus.

At the chosen place, the augur sat facing towards the west, separating his field of division into two parts. The place where he sat became the point from which the survey originated, the omphalos from which the four roads to the four directions were laid out. These roads were constructed upon lines which the corps of *agrimensores* surveyed. The line running north-south was called the *decumanus maximus*, and that which ran east-west the *cardo maximus*. These lines, which became the major roads of the district when constructed, were surveyed with one of the earliest surveying instruments, the *groma*. This was composed of a rod, pointed at the bottom for placing in the ground, which bore at the top two bars at right angles to one another so as to form a horizontal cross. Each end of the cross had plumblines for levelling. Sightings were taken along each of the crosspieces, and poles were inserted in the ground at intervals to range the line being made. With this simple but effective instrument, the surveyors were able to lay out vast areas in an accurate grid pattern.

The major units of the centurial grid were squares with sides of 20 *actus* (2400 Roman feet, about 776 yards) along each side. The dimensions were generally the same everywhere. The *cardo maximus* was finally made up into a road 20 Roman feet (RF) wide, and the *decumanus maximus* became the major road 40 RF wide. At intervals of 20 *actus* secondary roads were built only 8 RF in width. *Termini*, plain or inscribed boundary mark-stones, were placed at the intersections of these roads. Every fifth road from the *cardo* or *decumanus* was 12 RF in width. These roads each formed the boundaries known as *limites quintariae*. Like the *cardo* and *decumanus*, these were public rights of way, though in practice farmers frequently tended to plough them up.

Extensive tracts of land were laid out in this way, disregarding everything that was there before except the largest of natural features, which could not be ignored by even the Romans. By laying out huge areas, the authorities reordered the way of life of country people into a role subservient to the central authority – the government of the city of the district. Indeed, the omphalos divined by the augur was often the crossroads at the centre of the city.

Official religion, controlled from the city, was incorporated into the country's new layout. In the centuriated scheme, *compita*, wayside shrines, were placed at strategic crossroads. The scholiast gives the following account:

Compita are places in crossroads, a kind of tower where rustics perform sacrifices when the labour of the fields is finished. They are not only places in a city, but also on public roads, and are houses of refreshment for the inhabitants of adjoining lands, where little chapels open on all sides are consecrated. In the chapels the cultivators place yokes as evidence of their task being duly served and completed.

These *compita* therefore formed a sustaining grid of sacrificial points which were directly related to the divined origin point of the *cardo* and *decumanus*. The *compita* served to promote the fertility of the grid of fields, and largely supplanted all but the most powerful of ancient shrines. Even so, secular and sacred were still fused in a way almost incomprehensible to the modern mind, despite the reconstruction of the religious life of the country. Although the layout of land in clinical mathematics is largely unrelated to the natural features of the country, the reordering was carried out with the underlying intention of reflecting a form of natural order which the augurs believed to be inherent in the cosmos. Designed according to the auspices, the scheme was intended to enhance the natural world to the benefit of man and the state, whilst appeasing and placating the gods in the appropriate manner. The farmers' lives were still lived in a world where each facet of everyday life was an act of worship carried out in accordance with the auspices.

Centuriation was never applied to the whole Roman empire. In many places the old layout was retained and the ancient religious practices associated with it survived also. When Christianity became the official religion of the empire in AD 391, a concerted effort was made to stamp out all other religions and beliefs. Indeed, many early Christian ideas and beliefs which were thought to be dangerous to the empire were also extirpated as heresy.

In the urban context, the extermination of alternative creeds was rendered relatively simple. Pagan temples were either profaned or converted directly into churches. Pagan shrines were smashed and replaced with Christian ones. In the country, however, things were different. The ancient wells, hills and stones in non-centuriated areas were part of the country people's everyday existence and could not so easily be converted.

When the Roman empire disintegrated, urban life in the outermost countries all but ceased, and the populace in these areas largely rejected Christianity and reverted to their native paganism. Apart from *compita*, which were barely even chapels, temples did not exist in the countryside. In the classical Roman empire, temples existed only in cities, or at exceptionally powerful centres of the *genius loci*. It was not until several centuries later, when the reconversion of northern Europe was accomplished, that temples were exported to the countryside in the form of churches. This was yet another symptom of the urbanization process. Churches were erected in every village, symbols of the centralized power of the church which ultimately emanated from the Pope in Rome.

Although it died with the Roman empire, the practice of dividing the land in grids of great size was resurrected several times. In the seventh century of our era, the Kofuku towns were founded in Japan upon a system which has direct parallels with centuriation. The system known as *Jô-Ri* is identically conceived, with *Jô* as a north-south line intersecting *Ri*, the east-west line, with repeated lines at intervals to make a grid. After the Reformation in Europe, schemes of grids became popular as methods of reordering reclaimed lands and colonies. For instance, when the Beemster Polder, west of Edam in the Netherlands, was reclaimed from the sea in the first half of the seventeenth century, the engineers who accomplished the task laid it out in a grid pattern whose units were squares with sides measuring one nautical mile, within which a smaller grid of canals was made, each canal being one tenth of a nautical mile apart.

Another such grid plan was proposed by Sir Robert Montgomery, who in 1717 planned the layout of the colony of South Carolina in blocks 20 miles square. Inside these 20-mile blocks were to be cells of one mile square. This scheme was repeated for Ohio by General H. Bouquet in 1765. A variation on Montgomery's ideas were Bouquet's fortified one-mile squares, each of which had under its control five adjacent squares of arable land, woodland and pasture. Even grander than the previous two plans was that devised in 1784 by Jefferson and Williamson. Their scheme envisaged the 'centuriation' of the whole United States, which would have involved dividing the whole country into a grid of squares each with sides of ten geographical miles.

The systems adopted in Holland and North America were unlike that used by the ancient Romans in that their relationship with the earth was minimal. The Jefferson-Williamson plan was only related to the size of the planet through the use of geographical miles, whereas the metrologers of the French Revolution had a greater aspiration in determining the Metre. This measure was based on the earth's dimensions, so that each landholder could say of his piece of communal ground: 'By so much am I co-proprietor of the earth.'

The Industrial Revolution produced yet another kind of reordering. First canals, then railways forged their way across the country between towns, cutting traditional areas in half and altering the countryside for ever. Towns themselves sprawled towards each other,

The grid system which forms the layout of much of North America: a stretch of farmland west of Indianapolis, about eight and a half miles square.

finally merging in vast conurbations like the Ruhr and South Lancashire. Here, planning was largely absent and function was the chief guideline. The routes of railways were decided upon the basis of cost efficiency and already existing land tenure, and they had a decisive effect in disseminating urban culture into the country-side. The consolidation of the railways into networks also led to the imposition of standard time on whole countries. Instead of each place's time being determined directly from the sun as had tended to happen before, the necessity for scheduled timetables on the railways led to the imposition of one standard time throughout the country. Of all the world's states, only Saudi Arabia, which possesses no railway network and few cities, retains local solar time. Everywhere else is zoned – and these zones are determined by solar time at major cities.

Finally, in the twentieth century electrification has linked whole countries together in a unified power grid which reproduces in its fundamentals the power supply of a single city. The mass-communications media, too, link the remotest parts directly with the most central, disseminating a universal urban culture which threatens to annihilate local variation. Mechanization of farming has made even agriculture dependent upon the manufacturing capability of cities, and the automobile has largely displaced animals for transportation. Thus the urbanization of the countryside is now approaching completion in many places.

11

The city as image of the cosmos

And the City lieth foursquare, and the length is as large as the breadth: and he measured the city with the reed, twelve thousand furlongs. The length and the breadth and the height of it are equal.

St John the Divine, *Revelation* XXI, 16

The city, fundamental unit of human civilization, has always been a microcosm of its immediate world, containing within its boundaries the hierarchical structure of the society. The rituals and sacrifices which attended the foundation of cities in ancient times reveal the geomantic nature of their design. Owing to the terrain, to the political, economic and social developments, or to the vagaries of the natural environment, few cities have retained their cosmologically based format intact, having been enlarged or rebuilt according to different schemes. Despite these failings, an enduring theme throughout human civilization has been the concept of the Ideal City, a concrete expression of a cosmological idea which has been planned, founded, constructed and destroyed at many places and in many periods throughout recorded history.

Such ideal cities, cosmic cities or holy cities, for they have many names, have always adhered to one of a handful of plans. Their designs reflected both the cosmological and social orders, being expressions of the total civilization which they represented, including the ideal aspects of the architectural, artistic, astronomic, astrological, religious and political spheres of life.

In the case of the city states, city and nation were synonymous. The national territorial limits frequently ended only a short distance from the centre of the city, and sometimes at the walls themselves. Each city was the hub of its own world; each capital incorporated its own particular omphalos which was the centre of that world. From this centre radiated religion, trade, culture and directives, for, by its very nature it was centralist and authoritarian. Literally the hub of empire and the seat of civilization, the city's power of attraction faded the further away one travelled. A city which approached the ideal was Peking. Here the innermost Forbidden City guarded the omphalos – the ritual site upon which the emperor as embodiment of the empire sat. Surrounding the Forbidden City was the ordinary secular city, which in turn was surrounded by inner, civilized states of the empire. Outside these civilized states were the less civilized provinces, finally separated from the barbarians and outer darkness by the Great Wall of China. In this way the so-called 'Middle Kingdom' was reproduced in material form, reflecting the hierarchical, concentric concept of the world which Chinese cosmology upheld.

The omphalos at any point was considered the centre of the world, so it automatically defined the starting-point for a city. Because the Ideal City is conceived as a reflection of the world, divided into four quarters, it was natural that just as the world's four quarters are of different character, so the four quarters of the city should also be assigned their own special functions. The differing functions of the four quarters united within the whole of the city represent the unity of warring opposites fused within the archetype of wholeness.

The extreme antiquity of the quartered plan, which is overwhelmingly the most frequent image of the Ideal City, is shown by the ancient Egyptian hieroglyph for city, which is a circle quartered. At the crossing of the *cardo* and *decumanus* or the *Jó* and *Ri*, is the omphalos. At this point there stood an important marker, a stone, pole or cross in the centre of the market-place: a temple, pyramid or ziggurat representing the central pivot or holy mountain of the world. Cities such as Teotihuacan in Mexico, Peking in China, Bagdad in the Near East, and Winchester in Britain, all were laid out on the principle of quaternity. The fourfold nature of the city's division by the two roads is still reflected in language, even in cities which have been laid out according to other principles, or indeed according to none. Everyone has heard of the 'Latin Quarter' of Paris, the 'headquarters' of an army, or of the 'quartermaster' who laid out military camps and allocated stores and supplies. In all these cases, the derivation of the word 'quarter' is from the image of the Ideal City. In the military context it is derived from the layout of marching camps which followed the customary pattern for temporary towns like the Icelandic Althing, and echoed the quaternary concept of the world. Such layouts of Roman military forts, and their later development into towns, preserved this design which is still in evidence in the English cities of Colchester, Winchester, Chichester and Gloucester.

These towns were divided in such a way that each quarter was allocated a different function. Law tribunals and government offices were invariably to be found to the north of the east-west axis of the town, and the temples, military barracks and chief dwellings to the south. Such a pattern was faithfully preserved by the Saxons at Winchester and Chichester, where the position of the cathedrals occupied the correct sites for the main temples.

The specific position of temples and important buildings within a city was of course not merely for the convenience of planners, nor an ingenious method to ease the problems of visiting strangers. It was an integral part of a deliberate pattern ritually created to achieve harmony with the world – a state which had to be consciously achieved in an artificial structure like a city. The relation of these buildings to the four quarters was a conscious attempt to put them in their most effective position. The stability of the world was thus reproduced in the manner of sympathetic magic by the construction of an exact model (as they believed) of the universe. Standing foursquare, the temple or city was founded, like the world, in accordance with the plan of the Creator. This squareness was an assurance of permanence and absolute stability.

As the city was built in the image of the cosmos, so, in reverse, the image of the city was taken as the enduring symbol of God by St John the Divine in *Revelation*. Here the city was presented in the form of the cosmic cube beloved of templar and mason. The mystical city appears as the symbol of totality, the apotheosis of the Great Work. As the final image in human destiny, St John saw the descent of the Holy City to earth from the cosmos – the cubic New Jerusalem which ushered in the age of perfection and righteousness.

Just as the soul was held to travel through to the centre of the labyrinth by a spiral path to attain final enlightenment, so the Holy City, standing foursquare at the centre of the universe, represents the goal of the gradually progressing neophyte. Its four sides, facing the four directions, represent the four seasons of the yearly cycle, its twelve gates the twelve months or signs of the zodiac. That such an image should exist in such totally disparate cultures as the Khmer, Aztec, Sioux, Maya, Chinese, Hebrew, Roman, Hindu and Norse, attests to the common origin of all such archetypal images in the human psyche, and we need not postulate communication by reckless sailors to explain the similarities.

Through the Holy City, in whatever form it may have existed, a transforming fusion of mankind with the earth and higher powers was attempted. In being laid out according to the form of the earth (the so-called Four Corners of the Earth), the cosmological schemata combined not only the knowledge of the structure of the present world, but heralded the future. By creating it in this form, an early counterpart to the cosmic reality was made to await the new age.

Position of cities

The positioning of cities was always deemed of utmost importance, not merely from the admittedly vital considerations of trade, transport, water supply and agriculture, but also from the geomantic criteria of spiritual value, horizon landmarks, sacred springs and holy hills. Cambridge, for example, was set like Rome upon seven 'hills' (long since vanished). Durham's blind spring, indicated by the famous Dun Cow, formed the nucleus of the city. Dunstable was founded at the crossing of the four Royal Roads of England.

However, practical schemes were generally uppermost. The founding of the Egyptian city of Alexandria took place after Alexander the Great had rejected a visionary geomantic scheme proposed by Dinocrates. His plan had entailed the carving of Mount Athos into the likeness of Alexander's face and hands. The left hand of the vast image would have held a large city, and the right a water reservoir. Alexander turned down the scheme with the words, 'Just as a baby cannot nourish itself and grow without its nurse's milk, neither can a city without fields and produce flowing into its walls.' Instead, Alexander made Dinocrates plan the present city of Alexandria, incorporating harbour, city and fields as a single integrated unit.

The abandonment of existing cities and the resettlement of their populations in a more favourable place upon an alignment is on record as having been performed on several occasions. The most celebrated instance was that of the removal of the city and cathedral at Old Sarum to a new site in the nearby river valley, New Sarum or Salisbury. In this case, the alignment is the well-known line which links Stonehenge with Clearbury Ring. A century after the removal of Sarum, the Birke family in Bohemia laid out their fortified cities at equal distances along an

The Dun Cow of Durham: a carving on the cathedral records the incident which led to the selection of this site as a shrine for St Cuthbert.

alignment. Starting from a base at Leipa, they acquired Hohnstein, 28 miles away. A straight line connecting these two points crossed directly over the dominant mountain peak of the region, the Rosenberg, which divided the line exactly in two. In 1332, Hynek Birke, then the Chief Burgrave of the city of Prague, purchased the Bösigberg from King John of Bohemia. Birke ordered Bösig, the town at the foot of the Bösigberg, to be demolished, ostensibly because of the inadequate water supply. The population was resettled in a new town, Weisswasser, several miles to the southeast of Bösig, at a place directly on the alignment from Leipa to Hohnstein, and fourteen miles along from the latter town. It is interesting to note that one of the reasons for the removal of Old Sarum to its present site was that of poor water supply – perhaps a pretext for the mystical purpose.

The rise of the Città Ideale

Underlying much ancient expertise is the tenet that there is only one correct way of proceeding. To achieve an end, there must be an agreed form which, although able to expand and develop, cannot be permitted to depart from fundamental principles. Once these canonical principles are violated, then the system is weakened, disintegrates, and finally dies. The geomantic arts began to suffer this dissolution in the late Middle Ages in Europe, though elsewhere they survived until colonization and Western technical civilization spread outside Europe to the rest of the world. The disintegration of the old ways was accelerated by the rediscovery of classical modes of thought, and was finally made irreversible by the rise of science and its daughter technology, which has largely converted the world into a vast workshop-city. Thus Heinsch tells us that when new towns and cities were founded in Renaissance Germany, they were mostly held to be of 'illegitimate stock' as they had not been founded upon the geomantic principles of their forerunners. New modes had taken over, albeit based on cosmological principles, but viewed through Renaissance eyes.

Cities which have been planned and constructed as single entities have a unity which could never be achieved by piecemeal construction. Throughout history, such plans for ideal cities have been drawn up, usually to be discarded or at best only partially completed owing to changed circumstances. Renaissance Italy provides numerous examples of the Ideal City, or *Città Ideale*. Political, social, intellectual and economic conditions were ripe for the erection of such cities. Many of them were based upon the octagonal scheme designed by Vitruvius, with the contemporary addition of geometrical fortifications which had been necessitated by the invention and application of improved artillery. Such centrally organized radial cities expressed the power which emanated from the centre where the military tyrant had his tower or palace. Enclosed and protected from outside forces by a strong defensive system, the central fortress stood as a symbol of temporal power and the immobility of the omphalos about which all else revolved.

Centralized cities of this kind emanated from the drawing boards of great architects and planners: such cities were designed by Alberti, Filarete, Martini, Scamozzi and Vasari, among others. They combined the remnants of the medieval masonic sacred geometry with Renaissance mystical themes and solid military practicality. This connection between the masonic arts and military engineering is, despite its seemingly disconnected nature, part of the same tradition. In England from the Reformation, and elsewhere in Europe from the same period until the eighteenth century, military engineering was the preserve of a new kind of master mason. His geometrical skills were still merged with a knowledge of the landscape, albeit for a totally different purpose. Henry VIII's master mason, John Rogers, is a perfect example of such a transition from mystical architect to master of fortification. After all, it is not a great step from laying out aisles, transepts and apses by means of sacred geometry to designing bastions, ravelins, crownworks and redoubts. The mystical works of Robert Fludd show a pentagonal fortress, and pentagons, hexagons, heptagons and polygons of higher order can often be encountered today in many old continental citadels. This architecture developed from the basic forms of sacred geometry into the complex systems of the seventeenth-century military engineers like Errard, De Ville, Vauban and Coehorn.

As a logical extension of earlier forms of geomancy, the Italian *Città Ideale* was to a great extent limited, in an era of internecine strife, by the necessity for such military outworks. Despite this limitation, the designer of such cities merged the necessities of defence with the mysteries of sacred pattern. The city of Sforzinda, for instance, which was designed (1460–64) by Filarete for his patron, the tyrant Prince Francesco Sforza, was

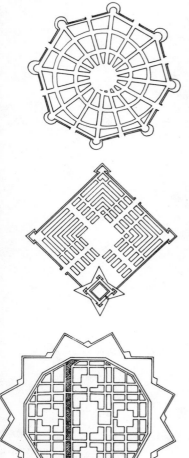

Ideal cities and the concept of war: above, plans for Renaissance ideal cities by Martini (top), Scamozzi and Schickhardt, with (top right) Robert Fludd's 1618 plan for artillery fortifications (De Munimentis).

based upon a Vitruvian plan in a defensive context. In the centre was a polygonal market place whose midpoint was occupied by an enormous tower, symbolic of the power vested in the autocratic prince. Named the House of Virtue and Vice, the tower was planned to be ten storeys in height, to contain a brothel and lecture halls, and, as befitted a geomantic centre, to be topped by an astrological college.

The city omphalos was marked by a 'holy hill' on the plan prepared by Martini (1439–1502). Again Vitruvian in inspiration, his city was octagonal with sixteen streets radiating from the centre. The central hill was ascended by a spiral road, thus incorporating the spiral pilgrimage motif of unicursal labyrinths within a Vitruvian plan, and achieving the centre from the perimeter in two and a half turns. But from a practical point of view, this was of advantage in the placing of artillery upon the hill.

Scamozzi and Vasari planned to build cities with a conventional grid of streets within polygonal fortifications, as was later done in the seventeenth century at Mannheim in Germany. Here a heptagonal citadel was superimposed upon a lower town of gridded streets surrounded by fortifications based on a decagon. One *Città Ideale* which survives today, Palma Nuova, was built in response to the very real threat of a Turkish invasion. In 1593 the Venetians built this fortress town with a ninefold radial street plan and a central fortified

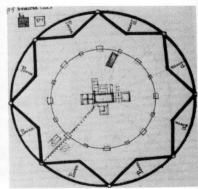

Left, *a* Città Ideale *which was actually built (1593) – the Venetian fortress-city of Palma Nuova, Italy, with its lines superimposed on pre-existing field patterns. Below, Filarete's plan for the city of Sforzinda.*

tower, but Palma Nuova is a 'plantation', with boundaries arbitrarily cutting across the former field layout and its positioning can thus be seen as an imposition upon the landscape rather than an enhancement of it. Its survival, however, affords us an insight which cannot be gleaned from published plans, however accurate they might be. Such fortified cities were unique both in place and time; events overtook them, and their era passed.

The city of Firuzabad, Iran, built in the first half of the third century A D. Its circular boundary, centred on the citadel rock omphalos, is crossed only by roads which radiate from this central point, linking the microcosm of the city with the macrocosm of the world.

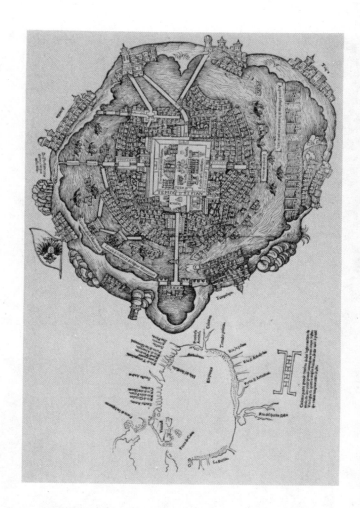

The first Western plan of the Mexican city of Tenochtitlán, constructed on the quaternity principle. The drawing is attributed to Albrecht Dürer or one of his brothers.

Later ideal cities

The image of quaternity was not used in Italian ideal cities, which tended to be based upon the octagon of Vitruvius. The quartered form did not die out however, and recurs in later ideal schemes. Albrecht Dürer, for instance, designed an ideal city based upon the quaternity plan, and some historians of art have even claimed that it was derived from the recently published plan of the city of Tenochtitlán in Mexico. But this is unlikely and can be explained since both follow a universal archetype. Heinrich Schickhardt (1558–1634) designed Freudenstadt in Württemberg in this manner, as a square with *cardo* and *decumanus*. In the centre there was a large arcaded square with a central palace, reminiscent both of the layout of Peking and of various Italian cities. The proposed Christian city of Christianopolis, designed by J. V. Andreae in 1619, again used the quartered square but in a well fortified setting. The mayhem of the Thirty Years' War on the continent and the Civil War in England destroyed the attitude of mind which had conceived the ordered ideal city in the form of the quartered square. After these traumatic events, new cities were of course founded and old ones reconstructed, but now they followed the Baroque form, based upon vistas and monuments.

Baroque cities need not detain us long, as the alignments which formed their major features do not appear to be significant in any way other than as optical devices. Admittedly Guimard, who laid out the upper town of Brussels in the eighteenth century, used alignments based upon the churches and St Gudule's Cathedral, but there is nothing here to indicate a geomantic rather than an aesthetic purpose. But Karlsruhe, built in 1715 on the orders of Karl Wilhelm, Prince of Baden, had a more deliberately mystical and symbolic design. At its centre is the monarch's palace, the central omphalos marked by a tower. Radiating from this tower, a series of roads subdivide the town and the Royal Gardens, while a circular road circumscribes the palace and gardens, with the radial roads continuing beyond. To the south of the palace, outside the circle, is the town, and to the north is parkland. The whole town and palace complex lies astride a road which is orientated due east-west with a parallel axis to the south of the circle. It is interesting to note in passing that the plan prepared by Albert Speer for Hitler's Berlin also used a similarly orientated axis.

The master plans of Albert Speer and his National Socialist contemporaries came to naught, perishing with the Third Reich. Since 1945, scores of planned cities and thousands of unplanned shanty cities have sprung up like mushrooms to cope with the proliferating world population, but those founded with visionary or mystic purposes are few. Lúcio Costa's general plan for Brasilia, the new capital city of Brazil, in the shape of an aeroplane, may be seen as the unconscious recreation of the native earth effigies of ancient America. The 'wings' are reserved for apartment blocks, the 'fuselage', together with the city's main axis, carries the ministry buildings, and the business and entertainment districts are at the central intersection. Unfortunately, Brasilia was planned totally for the motor vehicle, and its scale and layout ignore human needs to the extent of not even providing for pedestrian crossings on the racetrack streets. Although superficially geomantic, in spirit it is merely another of the desperately familiar new towns, created, as medieval

Germans would have put it, 'from illegitimate stock'. Other famous modern cities, like Chandigarh, though designed by the greatest talents among modern architects, remain different in spirit and execution from the holy cities of antiquity, based as they are upon an ethos of self-contained functionalism with little regard for the external world.

Most modern cities planned according to academic theories of aesthetics have failed to live up to the high hopes they generated when they were founded. Geomancy, which for so long emphasized the harmonious balance between humanity and nature may well point the way for a new symbiosis between the human race and the natural evironment.

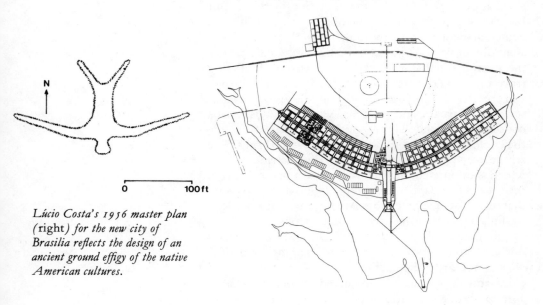

Lúcio Costa's 1956 master plan (right) for the new city of Brasília reflects the design of an ancient ground effigy of the native American cultures.

The end of geomancy

Yesterday heaven was the people's objective point; today it
is the earth. There are no more Crusaders, lance in hand.
Allah's scimitar rests in the museum showcase. The hordes
of the God of Israel are becoming atheists. The dust of
dogmas is disappearing before the breath of the years as
they go by.

> Ricardo Flores Magon, *Tierra y Libertad*.

A major distinction between the present era and earlier
periods of history is implied by the one fact that the
majority of the human race now live in cities. Urban
humanity is so divorced from intimate everyday contact
with the earth and its cycles that the modes of thought
which underly the practice of geomancy must now be
consciously cultivated in order to be comprehended.
The seasons and their aspects were formerly, in an
agrarian society, part and parcel of everyday existence.
Today, the average person is no longer conscious of the
equinoxes and solstices, or of the transition, other than
by the date on the calendar, from one season to the next.
The phases of the moon, so important to the natural
cycles of life, are only known from the stylized symbols
on the pages of diaries, as urbanization and its
concomitant construction precludes even the observation of celestial phenomena.

This inability to perceive the reality of the seasons
and our ultimate dependence upon the soil for our
sustenance has led to the erroneous belief that the
human race is now master of the forces which make life
possible upon this planet. So fundamentally have the
industrial, scientific and technological revolutions
transformed civilization that few can perceive that a
new reality has been created, and that the present differs
from the past not only materially but also spiritually.

The aim of geomancy has always been the re-
establishment of balance, the restitution of the cosmic
order by modifying human activity according to
complementary rather than contrary deeds. The dual
forces of construction and destruction have been
harmonized as far as possible. This striving for
harmony, which may be considered one aim of religion,

conceives of the world in a holistic manner, a continuum in which all acts and modes of existence are subtly linked by a system of correspondences. In this view, the performance of an act of any kind may have a perceptible effect upon the whole continuum. This idea is the basis for the ancient belief in sympathetic magic, the Jungian principle of synchronicity, and even the modern science of ecology.

Two diametrically opposed world views are represented here – the ancient holistic continuum in which each part is related and responsible to each other, and the particulate approach of the modern age, in which items can be isolated from the world and used without concern for the possible consequences. But 'The world is a holy vessel,' says the *Tao Te Ching*, 'let him that would tamper with it, beware.' The reductionist tendencies of modern science and technology have dismissed the possibility of such ideas, and instead have concentrated upon the cost effective plunder of the planet.

The strenuous efforts of people in earlier times, constructing gargantuan earthworks, aligning temples with minute accuracy, transporting huge stones without the aid of machinery, and removing cities to other sites, all attest to the exceptional importance which was vested in such ventures. That they are dismissed nowadays as the result of superstition and the megalomaniac whim of despots is a sure sign that they are little understood. But how has such a misunderstanding come about?

Like many a decline and fall, the loss of geomantic knowledge and expertise has been a slow and irregular descent. Certain areas of knowledge and expertise have always been the preserve of a small élite of specialists, and in earlier times this was no exception. Indeed, then there was a greater rigidity in society, with every person filling his or her ordained niche, whether king or serf, craftsman or cleric. The practitioners of geomancy were intimately interwoven with the fabric of society, and vulnerable to the changes within it. In a society which did not commit its knowledge to writing, continuity depended exclusively upon the continuity of the bodies dedicated to its survival. Perhaps because of such changes, the expertise of the megalith builders was totally lost by 1000 BC. The secrets of the later Druids also largely perished when that order was destroyed.

The basic knowledge of geomancy, transmitted orally among initiates, in England retained its underlying principles until the late Middle Ages. By the

The Souldiers in their passage to York turn unto reformers pull down Popish pictures, break down rayles, turn altars into Tables

The end of geomancy: churches are desacralized by Civil War soldiers in a contemporary engraving. Below, the ruins of St Joseph's Chapel, Glastonbury, provided inspiration for eighteenth-century poets, artists and landscape gardeners.

Reformation, the knowledge was in the hands of the operative freemasons. At this time, the patronage of the church was suddenly withdrawn from them, and the intellectual climate altered abruptly. The sacred buildings which had formerly been planned and tended with the utmost care suddenly became the butt of vicious attacks. Monasteries, once havens of learning, were suppressed. Their buildings were demolished for their valuable materials, and their treasures were carried away to enrich the aristocracy, who were busy converting monastic lands into country estates. Ancient knowledge, preserved in the monastic libraries, was destroyed as worthless. The manuscripts were sold for use as cleaning materials, for binding books, or even just tossed into the rutted Tudor roads to facilitate the passage of the aristocrats' carriages.

With this old knowledge so abruptly swept away, a new age could dawn. No longer was it necessary to keep certain areas of woodland to preserve the geomantic balance of the country – the trees could be felled for profit. Puritan fanatics defaced the mystical carvings in the churches which had survived the destruction of the monasteries. Ancient ceremonies which expressed the transit of the seasons – morris dancing, the maypole, secular fairs and even some religious festivals, were restricted or banned, and the Lord's Day was observed in compulsory silence and immobility. Devotees of the ancient arts were hounded and punished for practising witchcraft. Injunctions prohibited altars and images and, in 1571 and 1585, stone crosses were proscribed and torn down. Even Joseph of Arimathea's holy thorn tree at Glastonbury was hacked down in a fit of Puritan zeal.

As a direct result of this new desacralization of the world, the essentially Puritan discipline of science arose, and its impressive achievements were held by their authors to prove that this was the only road to an understanding of the essence of the universe. All other modes of consciousness were eventually relegated to the status of superstition by the new orthodoxy. Anything connected with the old days was categorized as being not merely obsolete but definitely bad. A typical sentiment of the period comes from Henry Wotton's *Elements of Architecture* (1624) where he rails against Gothic architecture: 'This form, both for the natural imbecility of the sharp angle itself, and likewise for its very uncomeliness, ought to be exiled from judicious eyes, and left to its first inventors, the Gothes and Lombardes, among other Reliques of that barbarous age.'

Other 'reliques of that barbarous age' were, of course, the corpus of ideas and practices we would now call geomancy.

The whole layout of the countryside was altered in the sixteenth century by the enclosures of vast tracts of common land. The people whose livelihood was thus removed by the appropriation of their pastures rose up in numerous rebellions against the squirearchy, but invariably they were suppressed with ferocious rapidity. No longer under the control of those with hereditarily received knowledge, the country was dissected and reconstructed according to other principles. The newly formed estates of the aristocrats were moulded by the new profession of landscape gardeners into aesthetic forms, only to be ploughed up and reconstructed according to the vagaries of fashion.

The wholesale destruction of trees by the enclosures and the Civil War altered the face of the country even

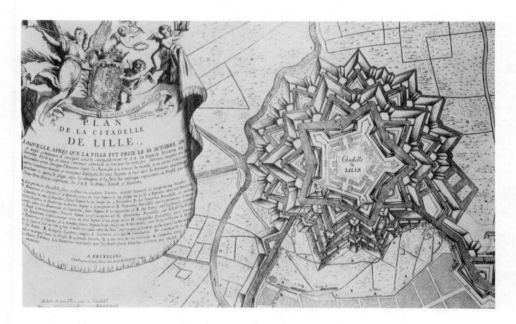

Geometry in the service of war: Vauban's fortifications at Lille (1709).

more. John Evelyn was so distressed with the situation that, under the patronage of King Charles II, he wrote the book *Sylva* in 1664, a treatise on tree-planting and forestry. These new trees were not direct replacements, however. The French influence on formal gardening, itself derived from Islamic sources, favoured the laying-out of vast avenues. Some of these actually followed old boundaries, but in general, new surveying defined their alignments.

Concurrently with the remodelling of the country-side, the transformation of architecture took place. The use of sacred geometry was confined, by the late seventeenth century, to the few educated architects who still had access to the old masonic secrets. The architecture of Sir Christopher Wren was still in the ancient tradition, but much work of later architects falls far short of the old canon. The average architect still had a working knowledge of proportion, largely based upon the teachings of Vitruvius and Palladio, but the esoteric gnosis upon which the arts of the cathedral builders of the Middle Ages was based was no longer available. Geometry was now largely applied to the field of battle, as military engineers refined the niceties of fortress construction. Sacred geometry retreated to the pages of Rosicrucian and other magical treatises, being finally committed to print as the fear of prosecution for heresy receded.

In the late seventeenth century, missionaries of the Jesuit persuasion visited China. Having gained the

The formal axial layout of buildings and gardens was epitomized by Versailles, seat of the Sun King, from whom radiated the rest of the nation.

confidence of the emperor, they attempted to stamp out Chinese geomancy, Feng-Shui, and by destroying many of the important books on the subject, they succeeded in mortally wounding it. Paradoxically, the influence of Feng-Shui was soon to be felt on European landscapes precisely because of this Jesuit mission. Versailles, which had been laid out according to a rectilinear plan by Le Nôtre, was, by the time of his death in 1700 beginning to be altered by the addition of sinuous paths and Chinese kiosks, ideas brought back from China in spite of themselves by the anti-geomantic Jesuits.

In England this Chinese influence, derived in outward form but not inward intent from Feng-Shui, was called *Sharawadgi*, a term applied to any non-geometrical picturesque layout of parkland. Such non-geometrical patterns rapidly became the rage, and ardent protagonists like Alexander Pope came close to the spirit of geomancy: 'All must be adapted to the Genius and Use of the place,' he wrote, 'and Beauties not forced into it, but resulting from it,' (*Argument to Moral Essays*, IV). The work of Henry Hoare at Stourhead comes into this category, when he erected a statue personifying the source of the River Stour as part of his rustic conceit. The name of Lancelot 'Capability' Brown springs to mind as the initiator of hundreds of examples of landscape gardening, many of which survive.

By the time of Hoare and Brown, the ethos of geomancy had receded from view behind a smokescreen of classical quotations, theories of the picturesque in art, the quaint in architecture and, even more fatally, the new cosmology of Kepler, Galileo and Newton. Ironically, many of these champions of designedly picturesque estates were in reality unconsciously destroying the ancient, geomantically derived patterns in the land. At the same period when landowners were commissioning 'Druidick' grottoes, Stonekiller Robinson and his spiritual brethren were busy uprooting megaliths which had stood untouched for 4,000 years. All over Britain, the old stones were demolished as taboos against their destruction faded into superstition.

The street plans of cities were drastically altered to accommodate avenues, initially constructed to provide aesthetic vistas, but ultimately to become, with Baron Haussmann in Paris and his imitators elsewhere, the means of rapid access for the military sent to keep down the populace. Canals and railways were of course constructed without regard for geomantic con-

Geomancy and 'the picturesque':
above, *the source of the Stour at Stourhead, Wilts, was guarded by 'the Nymph of the Grotto', while Neptune (*left*) provided another classical interpretation of the* genius loci *of antiquity.*

siderations, as their engineers had no idea of such concepts. Despite the use of a prehistoric mound at Blaencwm, Rhondda, as a survey point for the Rhondda and Swansea Bay Railway, and the laying out of Box Tunnel on the Great Western Railway by Isambard Kingdom Brunel so that the rising sun would shine through it on his birthday, there is no reason to confuse a convenient site or a whim with the conscious practice of geomancy.

Although often dismissed as superstition, or useless and unnecessary effort, or the caprice of eccentric individuals, some geomantic practice has survived in twentieth-century Europe. Some of the work of mystical architects such as Gaudí, Bragdon and Steiner incorporates a new interpretation of age-old arcane principles. Running counter to the dialectical materialism of the modern age, their deliberately spiritual works strike an unusual chord in those accustomed to the constant reiteration of a theme on a matchbox. Architectural textbooks relegate them to some convenient category such as *Art nouveau* or Expressionism, if they even bother to mention them at all. But the possibility that they were concerned with an invisible reality beyond the physical is rarely considered – such things are no longer the business of architects.

Geomancy is still practised in certain circles in Spain, as has been demonstrated by the recent location of Franco's tomb at the centre of the basilica of the Valley of the Fallen, a vast war memorial erected to honour the dead on both sides in the Spanish Civil War. This may not seem to be a particularly significant gesture until it is realized that the whole shrine, surmounted by a massive cross, is itself the geographical (and geomantic) centre of the country. The interment of the Generalissimo at that point in 1975 perpetuated the ancient tradition of burying the body of the founder of a new order at the omphalos in order to ensure the stability of his successors. Totally against the modern spirit, which regards all places as equally profane, this new example of geomancy in action has scarcely caused a comment.

However, this is an aberration from what is now the norm. With the rise of the scientific method and rationalism all other world views have been systematically, if gradually, whittled away until they have become alien to modern modes of thought. The average citizen of Europe or North America is now so far removed from a world in which geomancy was an everyday fact that it is difficult to envisage it as a natural part of life. Even in this technologically advanced

world, though, geomancy is still practised in Hong Kong, Taiwan, Nepal, Indonesia and certain parts of Africa. Although it is now in a truncated and degenerate form a considerable corpus of knowledge is still preserved. From this we have been able to draw parallels with the practices recorded in ancient Europe, and find a remarkable concurrence.

A certain world view of the past tends to unconsciously underlie the interpretation of antiquity, namely the rise of civilization in a direct, scarcely broken line with an accompanying increase in intelligence. This implicit faith, however erroneous, is deeply ingrained in the modern subconscious. In the light of this belief the discovery of advanced methods in antiquity has to be rationalized in accordance with the theory. This has given rise to all manner of speculations about spacemen having brought superior knowledge to savages, in the identical way that nineteenth-century historians believed the Romans brought superior knowledge and culture to the savage Britons. The possibility that their skills could have risen spontaneously and are not mere freaks of history is an unpleasant thought to those who have a vested interest in the theory of progress, now elevated almost to the status of faith.

Theories held as orthodoxy have a remarkable tendency to be overthrown and replaced by concepts which were formerly denounced as fantastic. The diffusionist theory, for instance, which stated that civilization and technology originated in the Near East and travelled to Britain via Malta and Spain, has recently been completely discredited by the carbon-dating revolution. This showed that the British megalithic sites with their advanced mathematics had existed long before their Mediterranean counterparts from which, according to the diffusionist theory, they were derived. In fact, the inhabitants of ancient Britain, far from being on a par with the Victorians' ideas of the Australian aborigines, were practising advanced mathematics, geometry and astronomy before the rise of the First Dynasty in ancient Egypt. This turnabout and its implications has yet to sink in to the popular consciousness, schooled to a belief in Julius Caesar's imperious attitudes.

Conditioned by the view that all that is not covered by the term 'rational' is unscientific and therefore not merely unworthy of study, but pernicious 'anti-science', archaeologists have ignored the study of geomancy. Quite apart from the problem of whether or not geomancy works, which is a different question, there is an attempt to deny that it was ever practised. Despite the evidence of countless research workers, unmistakable parallels with systems still in action, and documentary evidence, the study of geomancy is still on the whole regarded as a suspicious activity somehow bordering on a plot to undermine the fabric of scientific thought. New discoveries in the study of ancient geomancy are attacked with an almost religious fervour by those in positions of authority in the academic world, and while most academics would philosophically admit in private the essential incompleteness of all knowledge, in public they put on a brave show of omiscience, if not in themselves, then in the subject and their approach to reality.

As every scientist knows, the more one learns, the more gaps in knowledge stand revealed. Just as cherished theories in archaeology such as diffusionism and the supposed incompetence of megalith builders to draw proper circles have been shown to be erroneous, so today's orthodox certainties are equally capable of transformation, given a new insight. One can only present the evidence, however fragmentary, and draw conclusions from it. If the results are at odds with the accepted world picture, then the world picture must be redrawn.

The church as the Body of God.

Bibliography

ADAMS, DAVID 'The Black-Watkins Connection'. *Journal of Geomancy* vol. 2, no. 2, 28–9, 1978.

ADAMS, FRED. MCLAURIN 'Cosmothonia, A Pagan Art Science for the Magical Transformation of Earth into Paradise'. *Korythalia* vol. 5, no. 1, 1973.

ALLCROFT, HADRIAN *Earthwork of England*, London, 1908.

—— *The Circle and the Cross*, London, 1930.

ANONYMOUS 'Dragons Over Albion'. *Cymbeline* no. 1, 1974.

ARNOLD, L. E. 'Fire Leynes'. *Fortean Times* no. 22, 6–11, 1977.

ATKINSON, R. J. C. *Stonehenge*, London, 1956.

BAYLEY, HAROLD *Archaic England*, London, 1919.

BEAUMONT, COMYNS *The Riddle of Prehistoric Britain*, London, 1945.

BEDE *The Ecclesiastical History of the English People*, New York, 1968 ed.

BEHREND, MICHAEL *The Landscape Geometry of Southern Britain*, Cambridge, 1975.

BELLOC, HILAIRE *The Old Road*, London, 1911.

BENNETT, F. J. 'Meridional Alignments in Kent'. *South Eastern Naturalist*, 29–36, 1904.

BIRD, ALFRED J. 'Geometric Principles and Patterns associated with two Megalithic Circles in Wales', in *Britain: A Study in Patterns*, London, 1971.

BLACK, WILLIAM H. *W. H. Black: Pioneer Geomantic Researcher* (Collected works), Cambridge, 1976.

BORD, JANET *Mazes and Labyrinths of the World*, London, 1976.

BORST, LYLE B. 'English Henge Cathedrals'. *Nature*, 25 October 1969.

BORST, LYLE B. AND BORST, B. *Megalithic Software*, New York, 1976.

BUNN, IVAN AND BURGESS, MICHAEL *Local Curiosities*, Lowestoft, 1976.

BURCKHARDT, T. *Sacred Art in East and West*, London, 1967.

CAINE, MARY 'The Glastonbury Zodiac'. *Gandalf's Garden* no. 4, 1969.

—— *The Glastonbury Giants*, Kingston-upon-Thames, 1975.

—— *The Kingston Zodiac*, Kingston-upon-Thames, 1978.

CAMPBELL, IRIS 'Magnetism in relation to Prehistoric Sites'. *The Ley Hunter* no. 12, 1970.

CHARPENTIER, LOUIS *The Mysteries of Chartres Cathedral*, London, 1971.

COHEN, J. AND CALMAN, B. *Angkor: Monuments to the God-Kings*, New York, 1975.

CORBUSIER, LE *Modulor*, London, 1954.

COX, R. HIPPISLEY *The Green Roads of England*, London, 1914.

CRAMPTON, PATRICK *Stonehenge of the Kings*. London, 1967.

CRITCHLOW, KEITH *Order in Space*. London, 1972.

CRUMP, BARBARA 'A view on the South-West'. *The Ley Hunter* no. 22, 6–8, August 1971.

CURL, JAMES STEVENS *European Cities and Society*, London, 1970.

CYR, DONALD L. *Stonehenge Evidence for Halo Phenomena*, Santa Barbara, 1973.

—— 'Hidden Haloes found in Ireland'. *Stonehenge Viewpoint* vol. 6, no. 9, 2–9.

DAMES, MICHAEL *The Silbury Treasure*, London, 1976.

—— *The Avebury Cycle*, London, 1977.

DEVEREUX, PAUL 'The Forgotten Heart of Albion. Some Aspects of Leicestershire Lore'. *The Ley Hunter* no. 66, 2–4, 9–12, 1975.

—— 'UFO Leys: Alignment for Issue 75'. *The Ley Hunter* no. 75, 10–11, 1977.

DINEEN, FRANK 'The Underground Connection'. *The Essex Dowser* nos. 11 and 12, 18–22, 1976.

DUKE, E. *The Druidical Temples of the County of Wilts.*, Salisbury, 1846.

DUTT, W. A. *Standing Stones of East Anglia*, Lowestoft, 1921.

—— *Ancient Mark-stones of East Anglia*, Lowestoft, 1926.

DYMOND, C. W. *Stanton Drew* 2nd ed. Cambridge, 1976.

—— *The Hurlers: Cornish Stone Circles*, Cambridge, 1977.

EITEL, E. J. *Feng-Shui*, London, 1973, Cambridge, 1973.

ELIADE, MIRCEA *Cosmos and History*, New York, 1959.

FAROUT, F. G. *Astronomie Cambodgienne*, Saigon, 1910.

FORBES, JOHN FOSTER *The Unchronicled Past*, London, 1938.

FORREST, ROBERT 'The Mathematical Case against Ley Lines and Related Topics'. *Journal of Geomancy* vol. 1, no. 1, 10–14, 1976.

——'Some Metrological Ideas'. *Journal of Geomancy* vol. 1, no. 4, 72–4, 1977.

—— 'Metrology and Chance'. *Journal of Geomancy* vol. 2, no. 3, 66–7, 1978.

FORRESTER, S. 'The Gogmagog Hill Figures'. *Arcana* no. 4, 1972.

FULCANELLI, J. *The Mysteries of the Cathedrals*, London, 1971.

FURNEAUX, RUPERT *Ancient Mysteries*, London, 1976.

GADSBY, P. AND HUTTON-SQUIRE, C. *A Computer Study of the Megalithic Alignments of Land's End*, Barrington, 1976.

GERLACH, KURT 'Frühdeutsche Landmessungen'. *Germanien*, 1940.

—— '"Heilige" oder zweckmässige Linien über Böhmen'. *Germanien*, 1942.

—— '"Richt"-Linien durch Deutschland'. *Germanien*, 1943.

GODDARD, J. *Handbook of Leys and Orthoteny*, London, 1966.

GORDON, ELIZABETH OKE *Prehistoric London: Its Mounds and Circles*, London, 1925.

GRAVES, TOM *Dowsing*, London, 1976.

GREED, JOHN *Glastonbury Tales*, Bristol, 1975.

HARTLEY, CHRISTINE *The Western Mystery Tradition*, London, 1968.

HASWELL, MAJOR B. W. 'Leys traced by dowsing'. *Journal of Geomancy* vol. 1, no. 2, 31–2, 1977.

HAWKINS, G. S. *Stonehenge Decoded*, London, 1966.

HEINSCH, JOSEF 'Vorzeitliche Ortung in kultgeometrischer Sinndeutung'. *Allgemeine Vermessungs-Nachrichten*, 49, 1937.

—— 'Gründsätze vorzeitliche Kultgeographie'. *Comptes Rendus du Congrès International de Geographie*, Amsterdam, 1938.

HESELTON, PHILIP 'Fifty Years of Ley Hunting', in *Time for The Times To Come Together*, Hartlepool, 1970.

—— *The Holderness Zodiac*, Kingston-upon-Hull, 1977.

HITCHING, FRANCIS *Earth Magic*, London, 1976.

HOLIDAY, W. *The Dragon and the Disc*, London, 1973.

HUDSON, HERBERT 'The Meaning of Artificial Mounds and Mark Stones'. *Journal of Geomancy* vol. 1, no. 2, 24–9, 1977.

JOHNSON, WALTER *Byways in British Archaeology*, Cambridge, 1912.

JONES, INIGO *Stone-Heng*, London, 1655.

JONES, F. *The Holy Wells of Wales*, Cardiff, 1954.

JONES, PRUDENCE 'East Anglian Church Towers'. *Journal of Geomancy* vol. 1, no. 1, 1–4, 1976.

KIMMIS, J. *The Ongar Zodiac*, Cambridge, 1977.

KOOP, KENNETH H. 'Coldharbour Alignments'. *Atlantis* vol. 4, no. 4, 1951.

KROPOTKIN, PETER *Mutual Aid: A Factor in Evolution*, London, 1902.

LAWTON, ARTHUR *Mysteries of Ancient Man*, London, 1939.

LESSER, G. *Gothic Cathedrals and Sacred Geometry*, London, 1957.

LETHABY, W. R. *Architecture, Mysticism and Myth*, London, 1892.

LETHBRIDGE, T. C. *Gogmagog: The Buried Gods*, London, 1957.

—— *Gog Magog. The Discovery and Subsequent Destruction of a Great British Antiquity*, Cambridge, 1973.

LOCKYER, SIR NORMAN *Stonehenge*, London, 1909.

LORD, PROF. ROBERT 'Terrestrial Zodiac Research' in *Proceedings of the First Cambridge Geomancy Symposium*, Cambridge, 1977.

MALDEN, HENRY *An Account of King's College Chapel in Cambridge*, Cambridge, 1759.

MÂLE, EMILE *The Gothic Image*, London, 1961.

MALTWOOD, KATHERINE EMMA *The Enchantments of Britain*, Victoria, Nova Scotia, 1946.

—— *A Guide to Glastonbury's Temple of the Stars*, London, 1964.

—— *Archaic Sculpturings*, Glasgow, 1915.

—— *The Glasgow Druid Temple*, Glasgow, 1939.

—— *Craftsmen's Measures*, Glasgow, 1945.

—— *A Lost Civilization* (1927, unpublished, but the surviving fragments recovered by the Institute of Geomantic Research and published as an *Occasional Paper* in 1977).

MARK, ROBERT 'The Structural Analysis of Gothic Cathedrals'. *Scientific American*, 90–99, November 1972.

MASINI, LARA VINCA *Gaudi*, London, 1969.

MASSINGHAM, H. J. *Downland Man*, London, 1926.

MATTHEWS, W. H. *Mazes and Labyrinths*, London, 1922.

MCLEAN, ADAM *The Standing Stones of the Lothians*, Edinburgh, 1977.

MICHEL, AIMÉ *Flying Saucers and the Straight Line Mystery*, New York, 1958.

MICHELL, JOHN 'UFOs and the Message from the Past'. *Albion* no. 1, 1968.

—— *The View Over Atlantis*, London, 1969.

—— *City of Revelation*, London, 1972.

—— *The Old Stones of Land's End*, London, 1974.

—— *Earth Spirit*, London, 1975.

—— *A Little History of Astro-Archaeology*, London, 1977.

——'Statistical Leyhunting'. *The Ley Hunter* no. 74, 11–12, 1977.

MOORE, STEVE 'Feng-Shui and Leys'. *The Ley Hunter* no. 72, 1976.

MORTON, H. V. *In Search of England*, London, 1927.

MÖSSINGER, FRIEDRICH 'Baumtanz und Trojaburg'. *Germanien*, 1940.

MUNRO, ANDREW 'The Gogmagog Hill Figures'. *Cambridge Voice*, Series 2, no. 4, 1970.

NELSON, E. M. *The Cult of the Circle Builders*, London, 1909.

NEWHAM, C. A. *The Astronomical Significance of Stonehenge*, Leeds, 1972.

NICHOLS, ROSS *The Mysteries of Avebury – The Avebury–Stonehenge Axis of the Powers*, London (undated, probably 1965).

—— *The Timestones of the Druids*, London (undated).

OATLEY, KEITH 'Mental Maps for Navigation'. *New Scientist* vol. 64, no. 928, 863–866, 1974.

PENNICK, NIGEL *The Nuthampstead Zodiac*, Bexley, 1972.

—— 'Organic Metaphysics'. *Arcana* no. 3, 1972.

—— *Geomancy*, Cambridge, 1973.

—— *Caerdroia*, Cambridge, 1974.

—— *The Mysteries of King's College Chapel*, Cambridge, 1974.

—— *Leys and Zodiacs*, Cambridge, 1975.

—— *European Metrology*, Cambridge, 1975.

—— *The Geomancy of Glastonbury Abbey*, Cambridge, 1976.

—— *Ancient Hill Figures of England*, Cambridge, 1976.

—— 'Pioneer Researchers in Geomancy'. *Stonehenge Viewpoint* vol. 9, no. 1, 1978.

PENNICK, NIGEL AND LORD, ROBERT *Terrestrial Zodiacs in Britain: Nuthampstead Zodiac and Pendle Zodiac*, Hong Kong, 1976.

PENNICK, RUPERT 'Observations on the Book of Joshua and Related Events'. *Journal of Geomancy* vol. 1, no. 4, 65–71, 1977.

PONTING, GERALD AND PONTING, MARGARET *The Standing Stones of Callanish*, Callanish, 1977.

RADFORD, E. AND RADFORD, M.A. *Encyclopedia of Superstitions*, London, 1961.

REICHE, MARIA *Mystery on the Desert*, London, 1970.

REISER, OLIVER *This Holyest Erthe*, London, 1974.

REUTER, O. S. *Germanischer Himmelskunde*, Munich, 1934.

RIMMER, A. *Ancient Stone Crosses of England*, London, 1875.

ROBERTS, ANTHONY *Atlantean Traditions in Ancient Britain*, Llanfynydd, 1974.

ROBERTS, ANTHONY, ed. *Glastonbury, Ancient Avalon, New Jerusalem*, London, 1976.

RUDGE, E. A. 'The Conglomerate Track'. *The Essex Naturalist* vol. 29, 1950.

—— 'The Puddingstone Track'. *The Essex Naturalist* vol. 29, 1950.

—— 'The Statistical Evidence For a Conglomerate Alignment in Essex'. *The Essex Naturalist* vol. 29.

SALE, J. L. *The Secret of Stonehenge*, London, 1965.

SCHOLFIELD, P. H. *The Theory of Proportion in Architecture*, Cambridge, 1958.

SCREETON, PAUL 'Leys and Orthotenies Symposium'. *The Ley Hunter* no. 14, 1970.

—— 'Terrestrial Zodiacs: A Bibliography'. *The Oracle of Albion* no. 2, 1972.

—— 3 Northumbrian Zodiacs. *The Oracle of Albion* no. 2, 1972.

—— *Quicksilver Heritage*, Wellingborough, 1974.

—— 'Terrestrial Zodiacs Bibliographies' (cumulative in *Terrestrial Zodiacs Newsletter* (1977).

SEARLE, SIDNEY 'The Church Points the Way'. *New Scientist* vol. 61, no. 879, 10–13, 1974.

SHETRONE, H. C. *The Mound Builders*, New York, 1930.

SIEBER, SIEGFRIED 'Ein Trojaburg in Pommern'. *Germanien*, 1936.

SILVERBERG, ROBERT *The Mound Builders*, New York, 1970.

SOMERVILLE, H. B. 'Astronomical Indications in the Megalithic Monument at Callanish'. *Journal of the British Astronomical Association* vol. 23, 1912.

—— 'Instances of Orientation in Prehistoric Monuments of the British Isles'. *Archaeologia* II, 23, 1923.

SPENCE, M. *Standing Stones and Maeshowe of Stenness*, Paisley, 1894.

SQUIER, E. G. AND DAVIS, E. H. *Ancient Monuments of the Mississippi Valley*, Washington D.C., 1848.

STENCEL, ROBERT; GIFFORD, FRED. AND MORÓN, ELEANOR 'Astronomy and Cosmology at Angkor Wat'. *Science* vol. 193, no. 4250, 1976.

STIRLING, WILLIAM *The Canon*, London, 1897.

STUKELEY, WILLIAM *Abury Described*, London, 1743.

SYKES, EGERTON 'Baetulae and Ley Mark Stones'. *Atlantis* vol. 28, no. 6, 112–14, 1975.

TEUDT, WILHELM *Germanische Heiligtümer*, Jena, 1929.

THOM, PROFESSOR A. *Megalithic Sites in Britain*, London, 1967.

—— *Megalithic Lunar Observatories*, London, 1971.

—— *Carnac, Stonehenge, Brogar, Islay*. Offprints of papers from the *Journal for the History of Astronomy*. 1971–5.

THOMPSON, D'ARCY *On Growth and Form*, Cambridge, 1917.

TROLLOPE, E. 'Notices of Ancient and Mediaeval Labyrinths'. *Archaeological Journal*, 15, 1858.

TYLER, MAJOR F. C. *The Geometric Arrangement of Ancient Sites*, London, 1939.

UNDERWOOD, GUY *The Pattern of the Past*, London, 1969.

'VIATORES' *Roman Roads in the South-East Midlands*, London, 1964.

VILLIERS-STUART, PATRICIA 'Number Geometry'. *The Ley Hunter* no. 78, 12–13, 1977.

VITRUVIUS *The Ten Books on Architecture* (trans. M. H. Morgan). New York, 1960.

WARD-PERKINS, J. B. *Cities of Ancient Greece and Rome*, London, 1974.

WATKINS, ALFRED *Early British Trackways*, London, 1922.

—— *The Old Straight Track*, London, 1925.

—— *The Ley Hunter's Manual*, London, 1927, Bristol, 1977.

—— 'The Proof of Ancient Track Alignment'. *Antiquaries' Association Journal* vol. 1, 167–70, 1931.

—— *Archaic Tracks Around Cambridge*, London, 1932.

WEDD, TONY *Skyways and Landmarks*, 1961.

——'The Path', in *Time for the Times To Come Together*, Hartlepool, 1970.

WINTLE, DOUGLAS *The Old Straight Track Club*, London, 1948.

WOOD, H. G. *Ideal Metrology*, Dorchester, Massachusetts, 1908.

WOOD, R. G. 'Ley Dowsing'. *The Ley Hunter* no. 34, 1972.

WORDEN, IAN *The Round Church of Orphir, Orkney*, Cambridge, 1976.

WRIGHT, IAN 'Pointers To an Elusive Giant'. *The Ley Hunter* no. 45, 1973.

YATES, F. *The Theatre of the World*, London, 1969.

Sources of Illustrations

Index

Figures in italic refer to illustration captions